United States
Department of
Agriculture

Forest Service

Southern
Research Station

General Technical
Report SRS-123

Fire Managers Field Guide:

Hazardous Fuels Management
in Subtropical Pine Flatwoods and
Tropical Pine Rocklands

Joseph J. O'Brien, Kathryn A. Mordecai,
Leslie Wolcott, James Snyder, and Kenneth Outcalt

The Authors

Joseph J. O'Brien is a Research Ecologist, **Kathryn A. Mordecai** is an Ecologist, **Leslie Wolcott** is an Ecologist, with the USDA Forest Service, Southern Research Station, Center for Forest Disturbance Science, Athens, GA 30602; **James Snyder** is a Research Biologist with the U.S. Geological Survey, Florida Integrated Science Center, Big Cypress National Preserve Field Station, Ochopee, FL 34141-1000; and **Kenneth Outcalt** is a Research Plant Ecologist with the USDA Forest Service, Southern Research Station, Center for Forest Disturbance Science, Athens, GA 30602.

Front cover: *top left: gyrotrac in operation in pine flatwoods on St. Johns River Water Management District property in central Florida; bottom left: prescribed fire in pine rocklands, Abaco National Park, Bahamas; right: prescribed fire in pine flatwoods near Newnan's Lake, Florida.* (photos by Joseph J. O'Brien)

Product Disclaimer

The use of trade or firm names in this publication is for reader information and does not imply endorsement by the U.S. Department of Agriculture of any product or service.

Pesticide Precautionary Statement

This publication reports research involving pesticides. It does not contain recommendations for their use, nor does it imply that the uses discussed here have been registered. All uses of pesticides must be registered by appropriate State and Federal agencies before they can be recommended.

CAUTION: Pesticides can be injurious to humans, domestic animals, desirable plants, and fish or other wildlife—if they are not handled or applied properly. Use all pesticides selectively and carefully. Follow recommended practices for the disposal of surplus pesticides and pesticide containers.

This guide was funded by the Joint Fire Science Program grant 5-2-02.

July 2010

Southern Research Station
200 W.T. Weaver Blvd.
Asheville, NC 28804

Fire Managers Field Guide:

Hazardous Fuels Management in Subtropical Pine Flatwoods and Tropical Pine Rocklands

Joseph J. O'Brien, Kathryn A. Mordecai,
Leslie Wolcott, James Snyder, and Kenneth Outcalt

Preface

This document, "Fire Managers Field Guide: Hazardous Fuels Management in Subtropical Pine Flatwoods and Tropical Pine Rocklands," is intended to provide an overview of current techniques and tactics for managing hazardous fuels in the tropical and subtropical pine forests of Florida, the Bahamas, and elsewhere in the Caribbean. The information presented here was distilled from peer-reviewed literature, technical reports, and the experiences of on-the-ground fire managers. Managing fuels is complex and site specific. This guide is intended to provide only a broad introduction to currently available techniques, some well known and others newer and untested. The goal is to give the fuel manager options and food for thought, not exact prescriptions for specific fuel problems. A fire manager must always acquire appropriate training and seek guidance from colleagues and experts before applying an unfamiliar treatment or experimenting with a new, untested combination of techniques.

Contents

continued

List of Figures

List of Tables

Section I: Introduction

The Purpose of This Guide

Wildland fires are an integral component of the ecosystems of tropical pine rocklands and subtropical pine flatwoods. Fuels such as leaf litter and understory vegetation accumulated rapidly and in less than a decade can reach dangerous levels that can drastically increase fire intensity in both prescribed fires and wildfires. Land use changes in the regions occupied by these forests have resulted in the exclusion of fire from many areas that formerly burned frequently. Land development has resulted in a mix of land uses, some of which make fire management difficult. These changes have created challenges for both prescribed fire application and the mitigation of wildfire risks. Because of the immediacy of these challenges and the need for action, the Joint Fire Science Program Board of Directors called for a synthesis of recommended hazardous fuels treatments for use by the region's land managers and for educating others unfamiliar with particular issues of managing tropical and subtropical pine forests. This guide gives an introduction to current techniques and information.

The Geographic Scope of This Guide

This guide addresses hazardous fuel issues pertaining to the long-needled pine forests known as subtropical pine flatwoods and tropical pine rocklands in south Florida and elsewhere in the Caribbean Basin. We define subtropical Florida as the part of the peninsula classified by the Florida Climate Center as hardiness zone 10A, and tropical Florida as hardiness zones 10B and 11, or the areas south of Lake Okeechobee including the Miami Rock Ridge, Big Cypress National Preserve, Everglades National Park, and the Florida Keys (fig. 1). We describe these and the Bahamian forests as tropical for climatic reasons, although they lie north of the Tropic of Cancer. Though this guide focuses on the southern half of the Florida peninsula, much of the information presented here is relevant in pine stands throughout the Florida peninsula.

Characteristics of Tropical Pine Rocklands and Subtropical Pine Flatlands

To fully grasp the region's hazardous fuel problems and arrive at specific prescriptions for controlling them, a fire manager must understand the characteristics of tropical pine rocklands and subtropical pine flatlands. This section discusses the ecology, the endangered species, the fire frequency, and the fire seasonality of these forests.

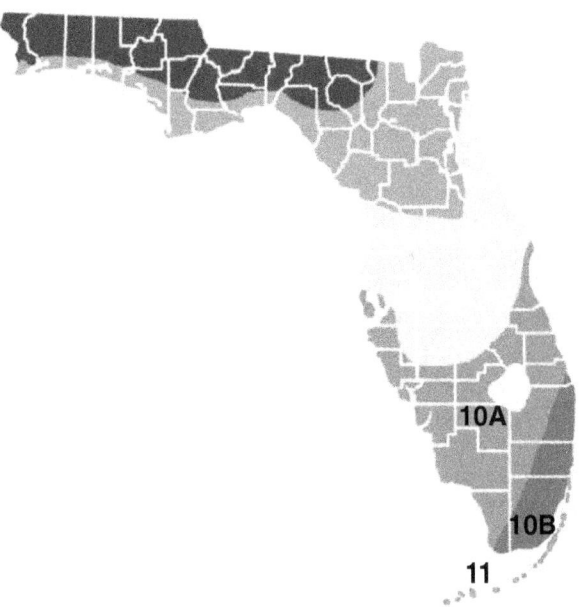

Figure 1—Map of Florida showing climate hardiness zones. Subtropical Florida covers the area in green (10A) tropical Florida occurs in the magenta and red areas (10B and 11).

Ecology—Both tropical pine rocklands and subtropical pine flatwoods are fire-dependent ecosystems. The characteristic fire regime for both types of forest consists of low-intensity frequent surface fires recurring every 2 to 10 years. When burned frequently, ecosystems covered in this guide share structural similarities, including a tall pine overstory (~12 to 25 m); a sparse midstory; and a species-rich understory layer of shrubs, palms, and herbaceous plants. Overstory pine species vary regionally and by soil type; Florida slash pine (*Pinus elliottii* var. *densa*) and some longleaf (*P. palustris*) and slash pine (*P. elliottii* var. *elliottii*) in the northern portion of the region form the canopy in subtropical Florida flatwoods, while Florida slash pine and Caribbean pine (*P. caribaea* var. *bahamensis*) occupy the canopy in rockland ecosystems in tropical Florida and the Bahama Archipelago. Other areas of rocklands exist in Cuba and Hispaniola with different pine species as canopy dominants, but likely behave similarly with regard to fire and fuels.

Tropical pine rocklands—Toward the southern tip of Florida, pine rocklands become the dominant pine forest type, differing from flatwoods mainly in substrate and understory plant composition. Pine rocklands are restricted to exposed limestone outcrops in southern Florida, the Bahama Archipelago, and parts of Cuba and the Dominican Republic. Amid the highly eroded limestone are irregularly distributed pockets of slightly basic soils of a mix of marls, sands, and clays. The type of limestone varies with location, with Pleistocene oolitic rock in Florida and the Bahamas, and older outcrops in Hispaniola and Cuba. The Floridian and Bahamian limestone is highly eroded and friable, making it susceptible to damage by heavy machinery.

Forest productivity, and, therefore, fuel accumulation rates, varies more with precipitation than latitude. Higher rainfall amounts, regardless of latitude, are associated with higher productivity, more frequent fire return intervals, and more rapid fuel buildup. The unique combination of soils, tropical climate, and frequent fires has resulted in the evolution of a diverse plant community. Roughly 30 percent of the plants found in Florida pine rocklands are endemic.

Pine rocklands were once extensively exploited for both timber and nontimber resources such as coontie (*Zamia pumila*). In Florida, the majority of the original area of pine rockland has been converted to other land uses such as agriculture and residential development. Most of the remaining Florida pine rocklands are in parks, wildlife refuges, and other protected areas. The Bahamas have the most extensive stands of remaining pine rocklands. These stands were once a source of timber, but currently are not harvested. Bahamian rocklands are actively being converted to agriculture, housing, and recreational developments.

Several endemic and endangered animals occur either obligately or closely associated with pine rocklands. Examples include the atala hairstreak (*Eumaeus atala floridalis*), Florida leafwing (*Anaea troglodyta floridalis*), rim rock crowned snake (*Tantilla oolitica*), Key deer (*Odocoileus virginianus clavium*), red-cockaded woodpecker (*Picoides borealis*), and Bahama parrot (*Amazona leucocephala bahamensis*). The community is particularly susceptible to invasion by exotic plant species. In Florida, Brazilian pepper tree (*Schinus terebinthefolius*), rose Natal grass (*Rhynchelytrum roseum*), Burma reed (*Neyraudia reynaudiana*), and melaleuca (*Melaleuca quinquinervia*) are particular menaces, since they alter fuels and impact the fire regime. Section III of this report provides more information on invasive species and their control.

Subtropical pine flatwoods—Subtropical pine flatwoods are savannah-like forests dominated by slash pine and longleaf pine and cover approximately 5.7 million acres in peninsular Florida. These forests, more extensive than pine rocklands, are found over sandy soils of lower pH in southern peninsular Florida. The structure of the vegetation is similar to pine rocklands with a pine-dominated overstory, a low midstory, and a species-rich understory. Highly flammable shrubs such as gallberry (*Ilex glabra*) and saw palmettos (*Serenoa repens*) dominate the midstory. Productivity is high and fuels accumulate rapidly. Many of the shrubs and palms have highly flammable foliage due to waxes, essential oils, and other organic compounds. Those unfamiliar with these forests are often surprised to see how vigorously the green vegetation can burn. Flatwoods-dominated landscapes are often a complex mosaic of uplands, wetlands, and savannas. Like pine rocklands,

these forests are species rich and have a high diversity of herbaceous understory species.

Some areas of subtropical pine flatwoods are still used for timber, grazing, and nontimber resources such as saw palmetto berries. Large areas of flatwoods occur in parks, refuges and other protected areas. Pine flatwoods are susceptible to invasion by exotic plants with several species changing fuel beds and increasing hazardous fuel loads. Examples include cogongrass (*Imperata cylindrica*), downy rosemyrtle (*Rhodomyrtus tomentosa*), melaleuca, and climbing fern (*Lygodium* spp.). More details on exotic species and their control can be found later in this report.

Rare and Protected Species

Many endemic or rare species of plant and animals are associated with Florida pine rocklands and flatwoods, with many protected by State and Federal law. Pine rocklands are especially rich in endemic species with many other examples of rare and endangered taxa found in the Bahamas, Turks and Caicos, Cuba and Hispaniola. Appendices D through G list the protected flora and fauna.

Fire Frequency

The rapid accumulation of fine fuels coupled with the swift postfire recovery of fire-tolerant palms and shrubs requires the frequent reapplication of fires or any fuel abatement treatment. The photos below (fig. 2) show how fuel loads recovered only 3 months following fire in subtropical pine flatwoods. The frequency of fire in these ecosystems ranges from 1 year to > 10 years, but the fires tend to be more frequent than less due to rapid fuel accumulation and abundant ignition sources. To keep fuel loads in check, fire return intervals should be < 5 years in subtropical flatwoods and < 10 years in tropical pine rocklands. Besides controlling hazardous fuels, shorter fire return intervals increase understory plant species diversity, lower fuel loads, and produce less smoke.

Fire Seasonality

Fire seasonality is a contentious issue within both the research and management communities. Many are in disagreement over whether fires ignited outside the high lightning season are "natural" fires. The disagreement may be moot since the contemporary landscape is unprecedented ("unnatural"), the climate is changing, and management guided by specific objectives is by necessity replacing management to achieve historical targets. Furthermore, human ignitions have dominated the fire ecology of the region for at least the last 200 years and likely as long as the 12,000 years humans have inhabited the region.

Figure 2—(A), 1-day postburn, Myakka River State Park; (B), 3 months postburn, same area. (photos by Ken Outcalt, U.S. Forest Service)

The landscape that today's managers have inherited was shaped by human ignitions.

There is no consensus on the impact of fire seasonality on desired management outcomes, partly because fire season and fire effects are often disconnected, i.e., high severity fires can occur at any time of year. The link between plant phenology and fire seasonality is also poorly understood, and no broad patterns have emerged among the plant species studied. Some species such as wiregrass (*Aristida stricta*) flower more after spring or summer burns, while others such as Big Pine partridge pea (*Chamaecrista lineata* var. *keyensis*) experience higher mortality after spring and summer burns. Furthermore, constraining all fires to a single season, whether dry or wet, will tend to homogenize plant community structure and composition. Until there is a better understanding of the seasonal effects of fire, a prudent manager might spread burning over several different times of year and monitor fire effects for desirable outcomes. Other practical factors such as fire weather, smoke management, and fire crew safety must be of primary concern when deciding to ignite a fire. Constraining the burn season necessarily limits burning opportunities, and if areas remain unburned, more fuel will accumulate and add to already hazardous fuel loads.

Section II: Fire and Fuels Issues

What Is a Hazardous Fuel?

There is no simple definition of hazardous fuel. Nonetheless, some criteria must be established to determine whether or not a stand is in a hazardous condition. Fuel loading, type, and arrangement as well as the surrounding environment determine whether a site should be designated as hazardous.

Fire managers of pine flatwoods and pine rocklands need to know about hazardous fuel categories, the production and accumulation of hazardous fuels, how to control the accumulation through prescribed burning, and how to deal with issues surrounding prescribed burning in the wildland-urban interfaces (WUI).

Hazardous Fuel Categories

Wildland fire experts in Florida generalize hazardous fuel threats into two main categories:

1. Fuels that create dangerous fire behavior
2. Fuels that foster smoldering fires and difficult smoke management

These fire managers further identified fuels that created threats to public safety and threats to natural resources. Fuels that present threats to public safety generally have a lower threshold beyond which they are considered hazardous than do those that present threats to natural resources. For example, forests embedded in urban areas create situations where fuel loads not otherwise considered dangerous in a rural context are defined as hazardous. In general, in defining hazardous fuel, managers refer to fire history, or the time since last fire, rather than metrics of fuel loading. The consensus of 50+ Florida fire management experts is that a hazardous fuel condition exists when there have been >5 years without fire in flatwoods or >8 to 10 years in rocklands.

Fuels that create dangerous fire behavior—Heavy fuel loads obviously can increase fire intensity and associated threats. Especially problematic is dense saw palmetto because both green and dead fronds burn with vigor. Also, when palmetto density and fire intensity increase, high pine mortality and low pine recruitment occur and can shift the ecosystem from forest to shrubland, as the palmettos are extremely fire tolerant.

Of particular concern is the presence of ladder fuels that can lead to crown fires and increase the potential for spot fire. Ladder fuels are found most frequently in long

Lygodium *as a ladder fuel in pine flatwoods.* (photo by Amy Ferriter, South Florida Water Management District)

unburned stands that have a tall understory and needle drape; stands infested with invasive plants; dense stands of young pines; and stands with dense palmetto, thatch, or silver palms (*Coccothrinax argentata*). Particularly hazardous ladder fuels are invasive climbing ferns.

Fuels that can smolder or create heavy smoke—A critical effect of any reduction in fire frequency in pine flatwoods or pine rocklands is the development of an organic soil horizon. In frequently burned stands, fire consumes litter and the mineral soil surface remains mostly exposed. In unburned stands, low litter decomposition rates, especially in xeric sites, results in the formation of a deep forest floor, with a thick duff layer, presenting a major problem for fire managers. Fires in duff smolder, are difficult to mop up, produce much smoke, and can reignite other fuels for weeks or months. Duff fires also can cause very high overstory pine mortality due to the loss of fine roots and damage to the bole.

Production of Hazardous Fuel

Accumulation rates of hazardous fuels in both ecosystems are fairly high and capable of sustaining very frequent fire return intervals of approximately 1 to 5 years. Fuel production varies with site productivity and rainfall; drier, lower productivity sites typically have longer fire return intervals. An example of fuel accumulation rates for flatwoods is shown in tables 1 and 2 below.

Pine litter is an important constituent of fuels, providing both a highly flammable fuel and creating continuity that can carry fire across vegetation-free patches. The relationship between basal area to fuel loading is shown below in table 2.

While shrubs and palmetto fuel loadings eventually reach a maximum, the litter continues to accumulate and a forest floor develops. A deep forest floor poses a particularly hazardous fuel because, when ignited, these fuels can smolder for weeks. Duff fuels are discussed in greater detail below.

In both ecosystems—rocklands and flatwoods—fire is part of a complex interaction with stand structure, fine fuel distribution, and pine regeneration. The overstory pines supply dead needles that create a critical fine fuel; because they are rich in flammable oils, pine needles are often the only fuel capable of carrying fire across vegetation-free patches of mineral soil or rock. In some longleaf pine forests, needles account for 60 percent of surface fuel mass. Additionally, pine needles can increase fire intensity when combined with other vegetation where fallen needles "drape" over less flammable fuels and promote combustion. Understanding the link among canopy structure, fire behavior, and pine regeneration is critical for forest managers regardless of treatment management objectives. When manipulating stand structure, a manager should

Table 1—Fuel loading relative to understory height and time since last burn

Understory height (feet)	Time since fire (years)							
	1	2	3	5	7	10	15	20
	tons/acre							
1.0	0.4	0.4	0.5	0.6	0.9	1.4	2.6*	4.2*
2.0	1.2	1.3	1.3	1.5	1.7	2.2	3.4*	5.1*
3.0	2.6	2.6	2.7	2.8	3.1	3.5	4.7	6.4
4.0	4.5*	4.5	4.6	4.7	5.0	5.5	6.6	8.3
5.0	7.0*	7.0*	7.0	7.2	7.4	7.9	9.1	10.8
6.0	10.0*	10.0*	10.0*	10.2	10.4	10.9	12.1	13.8

*Not likely to occur in nature.

Table 2—Fuel loading relative to stand basal area and time since last burn

Basal area (sq. feet)	Time since fire (years)							
	1	2	3	5	7	10	15	20
	tons/acre							
30	1.5	2.5	3.4	4.8	5.9	7.0	8.1	8.4
50	1.6	2.8	3.8	5.4	6.6	7.9	9.0	9.4
70	1.8	3.2	4.3	6.1	7.4	8.8	10.1	10.5
90	2.1	3.5	4.8	6.8	8.3	9.9	11.3	11.7
110	2.3	4.0	5.4	7.6	9.3	11.1	12.7	13.2
130	2.6	4.4	6.0	8.5	10.4	12.4	14.2	14.7
150	2.9	5.0	6.7	9.5	11.6	13.9	15.9	16.5

Duff layer development after 50+ years without fire. (photo by Morgan Varner)

Hazardous Fuels in the Wildland-Urban Interface

The WUI is probably the most serious issue facing fire managers working in the tropical pine rocklands and subtropical flatwoods. The WUI multiplies the difficulties, costs, and complexity of hazardous fuels management in both obvious and subtle ways. In a WUI, prescribed fires become more challenging and costly as an escaped fire could be catastrophic; taking the necessary precautions means a greater investment in equipment and personnel. Burns in a WUI generally must be smaller, thus increasing overhead. Policies governing smoke management can restrict the window of time for prescribed burns. In addition, because fire management activities necessarily take place in close proximity to the public, other hazardous fuels treatments such as mechanical or chemical treatments can face public opposition due to aesthetics or other perceptions about their impact. Managers working in the WUI must plan thoroughly for both treatments and contingencies in the event of a wildfire.

The WUI can be categorized by three main geographical types. Each category presents unique issues for the hazardous fuels manager.

- Boundary WUI. Land uses incompatible with or at risk from wildland fire occur along the boundaries of wildlands. The boundary can be clearly defined.

- Intermix WUI. Land uses or structures at risk are interspersed within the wildland. The boundaries between wildland and other land uses are indistinct. The proportion of wildland to nonwildland occurs as a gradient. There is often a checkerboard of land ownership and jurisdictions.

- Island WUI. Wildlands exist as islands embedded in a matrix of nonwildland.

Issues for Fire Managers in the Wildland-Urban Interface

Firefighting tactics—Structural and wildland firefighting tactics must be combined when working in the WUI. These tactics have fundamental differences. Structural firefighting tactics center on direct fire attack, usually with water or foam, while wildland firefighting generally focuses on indirect attack through the creation of fuel breaks. When wildland fires reach the WUI, wildland and structural firefighters must work as a team, and it is critical that all parties understand the tactics and techniques unique to each type of firefighting. Since the training and equipment for structural and wildland firefighters have been developed

consider potential impacts on fire behavior and subsequent ecological effects, not only on pine regeneration but also on other fire-dependent elements of biodiversity such as the herbaceous flora and snags that are important to wildlife.

Accumulation of Hazardous Fuels

Fire management in Florida has become hampered by urban encroachment; smoke management issues (how best to minimize public health and welfare impacts of smoke from managed fires, especially near urban areas and highways); and forest fragmentation. For these and other reasons, fire has been excluded from many stands, resulting in a buildup of dangerous fuel loads that are leading to recurrent destructive wildfires. Land use changes have established a complex landscape of areas incompatible with fire interspersed with forested areas, including islands of forests inside urban and suburban development. Once-continuous tracts of forest are now fragmented by new roads, land development, and agriculture. These land use changes coupled with a legacy of fire suppression have decreased the frequency of fires and increased the area of lands with hazardous fuels. This matrix of land uses is often referred to as the WUI.

to support the tactical goals inherent in each form of firefighting, understanding how to effectively and safely integrate these resources must be developed prior to any fires.

Jurisdiction—The WUI often exists as a checkerboard of ownership and jurisdictions. When treating hazardous fuels or suppressing fire, a number of agencies within the WUI must cooperate with one another for efficient management of issues ranging from command and control to payment for services rendered. Confusion over jurisdictional boundaries can lead to tactical issues. Responsibilities should be clearly established prior to a crisis situation.

Access—Depending on the level of land development, some WUI areas may not have the transportation infrastructure to support access by firefighting equipment. For example, roads may be too narrow for fire trucks, bridges may not support the weight of heavy equipment, and dead-end roads may create dangerous situations or limit egress following an evacuation order.

Water supply—Proximity to a reliable water source or municipal water system in the WUI is a boon for both prescribed fire and fire suppression activities. Water sources should be identified when planning these activities.

Prescribed Fire as a Hazardous Fuel Treatment

Fire is an ecological imperative in pine rocklands and flatwoods. Without fire, dangerous fuel loads accumulate and eventually plant succession will result in the replacement of pine stands with other vegetation types. When dealing with a legacy of fire exclusion or other fuel hazards such as exotic plants species, other fuel reduction techniques can have great utility in preparing a stand for the reintroduction of the practice of prescribed fire. While these alternatives can be effective in abating fuel hazards, there is no ecological equivalent to fire, and each nonfire technique will have tradeoffs.

Detailed prescriptions for using fire as a hazardous fuel treatment will not be dealt with here. This is due to extreme complexity and danger associated with using fire as a fuel reduction technique when fuels have become hazardous. Fuels are called hazardous for a reason: they can create the conditions for extreme fire behavior, fire severity, and loss of life and property. Burning a stand with hazardous fuels is the purview of experts. Appendix B lists agencies that can guide a forest manager to experts with the experience and skill necessary to use fire in managing hazardous fuels. Appendix C lists guides, certifications, and literature on safely and effectively using fire in tropical and subtropical

pine flatwoods and rocklands. We do not imply that fire is not useful in treating hazardous fuels; in fact, fire can often be the best treatment option. But its inherent risk requires detailed consultation with experts and careful planning.

Once fuel hazards are abated, a regular program of prescribed fire or wildland fire use must be established to control fuels and maintain these fire-dependent ecosystems, regardless of initial abatement tactics. Many times, other options such as mechanical or chemical treatments are more suitable for returning a stand to a condition where the ecological benefits associated with frequent fires can be realized. Whether or not fire itself is the best option for initially reducing hazardous fuels is complicated by many factors, such as ability to contain an escape, presence of the WUI, potential damage to the natural resource being restored, and smoke production.

- Pros:
  - Most ecologically appropriate treatment
  - Generally most cost-effective option
- Cons:
  - Danger of escape
  - Risk to personnel
  - Nuisance smoke and ash
- Length of effectiveness/retreatment intervals:
  - Usually need to burn at least every 3 to 5 years in flatwoods or 5 to 10 years in rocklands

Planning Prescribed Fires

All prescribed fires require careful planning, but working in areas with hazardous fuels requires extremely careful preparation. Planning a prescribed burn must conform to 2008 Florida Statutes Chapter 590 and Florida Administrative Code, Chapter 5I–2. The administrative code outlines a Certified Prescribed Burn Manager Program, administered by the Florida Division of Forestry (DOF) that provides liability protection from problems that might arise from a certified burn. Becoming a Florida Certified Prescribed Burn Manager would be wise for anyone performing prescribed fires, especially for those working in hazardous fuels. Fire managers may become Florida DOF-certified following successful completion of a comprehensive training program. Be aware that local rules might be more stringent than State or Federal rules, and that fire managers must be well versed in all applicable fire regulations. The following information must be checked against current statutes and regulations.

Regulations on Prescribed Fires

Current State regulations require that all prescribed fires, whether lit by a certified burner in Florida or not, must comply with the following rules:

- A permit must be granted by the Florida DOF. The permit must be in writing if there is a severe drought emergency.

- Adequate fire breaks must be established around the planned burn area, and sufficient personnel and firefighting equipment for controlling the fire must be on the burn site.

- Personnel must remain on site until the fire is extinguished.

- The burner must have the landowner consent.

- The fire must not escape the permitted burn area.

Certified burns have these additional requirements:

- A detailed written prescription must be prepared prior to authorization and a copy of the plan available onsite. The plan includes location, size, and description of the area to be burned; amount and type of vegetation; planned ignition patterns; acceptable weather conditions; responsible personnel; safety; and contingency plans for smoke.

- A certified prescribed burn manager must be onsite from ignition to completion of the burn and have a copy of the approved written prescription in possession.

- Florida DOF also requests that certified burners notify adjacent residents of the planned burn and follow up with burn results.

Factors to Consider in Producing a Prescribed Fire

In general, when working in hazardous fuels, burns should be kept as small as feasible because smaller burns are easier to control and produce less smoke. In producing a prescribed fire, fire managers need to consider ignition techniques, crown scorch, wildlife mortality, wildlife nesting and reproduction, habitat diversity, nighttime burning, fuel arrangement, smoke management, fire weather forecasting, and the use of fire behavior prediction models and other tools.

Ignition techniques—Often, ignition technique will be constrained by smoke management requirements or by proximity of the burn unit to other land uses. Many times, backing fires must be lit repetitively off the same control lines. This can have undesirable results such as the development of an "edge hedge" where shrubs and palms are not consumed by the low-intensity fires and form a zone of heavy fuels adjacent to the firebreaks. Corners where lines meet are especially susceptible to edge hedge development. Several managers surveyed used mechanical treatments successfully to abate these fuels.

Crown scorch—All pines in rocklands and flatwoods are resilient to crown scorch, and mortality is generally low even with 100-percent scorch. While crown scorch is often unavoidable, scorch is a stressor and aesthetically unappealing, and so should be kept to a minimum.

Wildlife mortality—Avoid ignition patterns that result in ringing fires so as to provide an avenue for wildlife egress.

Wildlife nesting and reproduction—Consider the reproductive phenology of species of concern when timing prescribed fires.

Habitat diversity—If possible, plan ignitions to create a mosaic of different burn ages and intensities.

Night burning—Nighttime burning is permitted in portions of the areas covered by this guide under special circumstances and conditions (fig. 3). Burning at night

Figure 3—Special case night burn areas. (from Florida Department of Agriculture and Consumer Services maps)

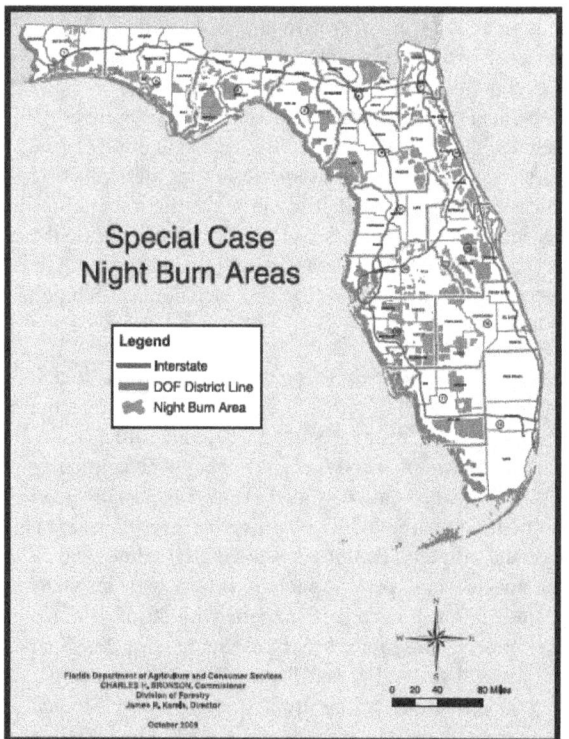

can limit fire intensity but can also create problems of smoke dispersion. Contact the Florida DOF for specific requirements on night burns.

Control lines—Exploiting natural or existing firebreaks whenever possible is a Best Management Practice. New fire line construction should minimize impacts to sensitive areas such as streams or riparian areas, follow topographic contours, and minimize erosion and sedimentation. When new fire lines are established, managers must exercise care that exotic plant species aren't established. Exotics can quickly negate the effectiveness of a control line because their rapid establishment can create sufficient fuels to carry fire. Ensure that equipment is seed free. Periodic herbicide treatment on the lines likely will be necessary to control invasive species that invade the disturbance. In areas with sufficient soil, disking a control line whenever possible instead of plowing minimizes soil disturbance and prevents disruption of surface hydrology. Control line establishment in pine rocklands is more difficult because of the limestone substrate. Permanent lines can be created using bulldozers, but this method has a high impact on the land because it permanently alters the structure of the limestone and creates rubble that can be points of entry for invasive plant colonization. Black lining, string trimmers, and hand raking/chopping are alternatives in pine rocklands, although these methods have significant drawbacks, such as fire escape risks and high labor outlays.

Fuel arrangement—Fuel arrangement has a large effect on fire behavior. Mosaics of different fuel loads can lead to unanticipated fire behavior. In the example shown below (fig. 4), a small fuel-free patch in the midst of continuous fuels created a patch of higher intensity fire in its wake. The headfire split into two flanking fires that then recombined with higher intensity as their plumes began to interact. This pattern appears to occur across scales, from pocket gopher mounds to clearcuts. A major concern for managers is that this phenomenon could initiate crown fires.

Altering fuel arrangement must be carefully considered. Fire managers in the Florida Keys have had success interrupting fuel continuity and reducing fire intensity by using mechanical treatments prior to burning. In that case, the machine created multiple continuous strips of compact fuels that snaked through the stand. There is ongoing research on how different fuel arrangements influence fire behavior, but fire managers should be aware that fuel arrangement can have unanticipated impacts on fire intensity.

Burning areas with duff—Restoring fire into areas with heavy duff is difficult but not impossible, and requires careful planning and narrow prescription windows. The duff must be moist enough not to ignite, yet the surface fuels must be sufficiently dry to burn. The objective of restoration fires in heavy duff is not to burn off the duff, but to remove undecomposed litter and prevent further duff accumulation. When litter input is consistently removed, decomposition will slowly begin to remove the duff layer. Restoration of stands with deep duff is a long-term proposition and must be approached cautiously to avoid smoldering fires and subsequent high tree mortality.

Though difficult to apply, fire is the best option for removing duff. Other methods such as raking are not practical over large areas, and some managers have observed tree mortality from raking that rivals mortality in stands where duff had burned. Since trees invest a significant portion of their fine roots into the duff layer, the destruction of these roots by fire or raking can cause fatal stress to the trees.

Fire Weather Forecasting

Fire weather is one of the most important as well as one of the most variable factors facing prescribed fire managers. The Florida DOF Web site provides access to a variety of fire weather forecasting resources for prescribed fire managers.

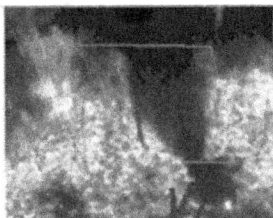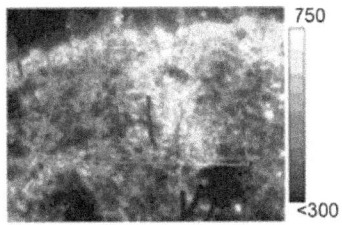

Figure 4—Three images of a headfire crossing a 5- by 5-m experimental plot in a longleaf pine stand. The images were collected every 30 seconds. Higher temperatures appear as warmer colors with white being 750 °C. A mound of sand on the lower right border of the plot breaks the headfire into two flanking fires.

Spot weather forecasts augment fire weather forecasts produced by the National Weather Service. They are available from 8 a.m. to 8 p.m. everyday and are generated by a numerical weather prediction model developed by Pennsylvania State University and the National Center for Atmospheric Research. To generate a spot forecast, users must know the site latitude/longitude in decimal degrees or the township, section, and range numbers. Users then input onsite weather observations of temperature, relative humidity, and wind speed and direction, along with the time of the observation. The spot forecasts then provide hourly predictions of temperature, relative humidity, and wind speed and direction.

Keetch-Byram Drought Index—The Keetch-Byram Drought Index is an index of fuel and duff dryness. The scale ranges from 0 to 800, with higher values indicating increasing wildfire risk. The index increases with consecutive days without rain. The index assumes that 8 inches of moisture represents a saturated soil. The minimum soil depth required to hold 8 inches of moisture depends on the soil type; the minimum depth for sandy soil, for example, is 30 inches.

Mesoscale Numerical Forecast Model—Mesoscale Numerical Forecast Model regional forecasts are generated by numerical models for 7 km and 21 km. Weather information is supplied as surface and upper air maps, as well as graphics of soundings and cross sections for selected locations. Soundings and 21-km maps are available every 6 hours over a 48-hour period, while the 7-km maps and cross sections are available every 2 hours for 24 hours. Soundings show vertical profiles of temperature, moisture, and winds, while the cross sections show vertical slices of wind, relative humidity, and temperature.

Live fuel moisture readings—Live fuel moistures for several sites, available from the Florida DOF, can assist in planning prescribed burns.

Other fire weather products are available based on observations and radar and satellite data from the Forest Service, National Weather Service, Florida Automated Weather Network, and Florida DOF.

Fire behavior prediction models—Several modeling tools are available for the prescribed fire manager. These models are frequently updated, and managers should check with the National Interagency Fire Center for the latest versions.

All models have inherent limitations and are only as good as the quality of the data that goes into them. Managers would do well to interpret the results carefully. As well, managers should keep in mind that models currently available for field deployment often fail under changing weather conditions or in mosaics of different fuels. Models under development hold promise for improvements in predicting fire behavior in these conditions.

Three widely employed models are BehavePlus, FARSITE, and First Order Fire Effects (FOFEM). These models require training to be effectively implemented but can augment the experience of a fire manager who is planning a burn. These programs can be downloaded from the Fire.org Web site, where the descriptions below were taken from.

BehavePlus—The BehavePlus fire modeling system is a PC-based program that comprises several models that describe fire behavior, fire effects, and the fire environment. A flexible system that produces tables, graphs, and simple diagrams, BehavePlus can be used for a multitude of fire management applications. As the successor to the BEHAVE fire behavior prediction and fuel modeling system, the BehavePlus system has an expanded scope of applications, and development continues with the addition of fire modeling capabilities and features that facilitate application.

FARSITE—The FARSITE Fire Area Simulator is a program for PCs that simulates the growth and behavior of a fire as it spreads through variable fuel and terrain under changing weather conditions. Operation and application of the FARSITE Program is taught in a national, interagency course (S493). FARSITE is designed for professional use, particularly by wildland fire planners and managers who understand fuels, weather, topography, wildfire situations, and other associated concepts and terminology of fire management. For example, the program is used by fire behavior analysts in the Forest Service, the National Park Service, the Bureau of Land Management, and the Bureau of Indian Affairs.

FOFEM—The FOFEM is a computer program developed to meet the needs of resource managers, planners, and analysts in predicting and planning for fire effects.

Smoke management—Concerns over smoke were ubiquitous among the fire managers consulted during the preparation of this guide. How smoke behaves is a critical issue in prescribed fires. Land managers, regulatory agencies, and the public must work together to form long-term solutions that maintain fire-adapted ecosystems while protecting adjoining landowners and the public from the dangers of smoke production. Smoke can reduce visibility on roads and endanger motorists, and can contribute to poor air quality across the region. Clearly understanding how fire weather affects smoke plume dispersion and settling is critical. To keep smoke under control, managers should:

- Minimize fuel loads prior to burning

- Burn when weather and fuel moisture conditions will minimize smoke production

- Complete burns as quickly as possible

- Notify the public and public safety officials of the upcoming burn

- Keep the public informed that minimizing smoke impacts is a management priority

Smoke management models—The Florida DOF has made an Internet-based smoke management tool available for use by prescribed fire managers at http://flame.fl-dof. com/wildfire/tools_sst.html. The Smoke Screening Tool produces a forecast map of smoke plume trajectory and characteristics from a planned burn. Prescribed burners should become familiar with other indices such as the Atmospheric Dispersion Index that predict smoke plume behavior. Managers must remember that weather conditions amenable for smoke dispersal might cause extreme or unpredictable fire behavior. Balancing these two effects requires considerable skill and experience.

Interpretation of daytime ADI values

ADI	Description
0–20	Poor dispersion, stagnant if persistent
21–40	Poor to fair, stagnation may be indicated if accompanied by low-wind speeds
41–60	Generally good
61–80	Very good dispersion, control problems likely
80+	Excellent dispersion, control problems expected

ADI = Atmospheric Dispersion Index.

Interpretation of nighttime ADI values

ADI	Description
0–2	Poor
3–4	Poor to fair
5–8	Good
8+	Very good

ADI = Atmospheric Dispersion Index.

Public Perception of Prescribed Fire

Studies have shown that there is a high acceptance of prescribed fire among the public, especially if the public is well informed on burning techniques and the benefits of controlled and prescribed burning. Public outreach is especially critical in the WUI. Professionals in the forest community must spend time with the public and continue working on helping people understand that prescribed fire is an important and safe forest management tool.

Costs of Prescribed Fire

Typical costs are $10 to $20 per acre with higher cost in complex burns.

Section III: Mechanical Fuel Treatment

Mechanical treatments in this guide are broadly defined as those methods that use machines (generally wheeled or tracked) to alter fuel arrangement and load. This category can be subdivided into roller chopping, mastication (mulching), thinning (with or without removal or piling), and mowing. These treatments are generally more expensive than prescribed fire and often have high impacts on nontarget vegetation. Mechanical treatments, though expensive, provide immediate reduction of standing fuel loads. These techniques are most often applied in the WUI or to prepare a long unburned stand for a prescribed fire. The number of manufacturers and types of equipment available for mechanically altering fuels is increasing and ranges from attachments for existing equipment to dedicated fuel treatment devices. Examples offered in this guide imply no endorsement.

Best Management Practices of Mechanical Fuel Treatment

Most managers use mechanical treatments as a preparation for prescribed fires or where fire use might be impossible. Uses include creating fire lines, reducing ladder fuels, or knocking down midstory fuels in long unburned sites to reduce fire intensity.

Selecting a Mechanical Fuel Treatment Method

The many options available vary by region. In Florida, most managers focus on a few types of treatments: thinning, roller chopping, mastication, and mowing.

Thinning—Thinning involves partial harvesting of select trees within a stand. This can be done for economic gains from the harvested trees, to accelerate the growth of the trees left standing, to reduce the crown cover, to remove invasive trees, or to bring equipment into a stand. Thinning can be accomplished by wheeled or tracked machinery or by hand with chainsaws. In hand thinning, some mangers have reported success when trees are flush cut and left to lay and then burned within about 6 months. This technique results in little or no soil disturbance and ancillary damage as sawyers can pick and choose what gets cut and what stays. Hand thinning is dangerous and slow, a four-man crew can treat between 1 to 5 acres a day, depending on tree density of the treated area. At the Disney Wilderness Preserve and

Feller buncher. (photo by Chris Schnepf, University of Idaho)

the Lake Wales Ridge State Forest, contract saw crews have had good results thinning dense slash pine regeneration and unmarketable planted Florida slash pine in long unburned flatwoods communities. For successful mechanical treatment, followup treatment with fire is imperative.

- Pros:
  - Effectively reduces live fuels
- Cons:
  - Can increase surface fuels such as downed trees or limbs unless they are removed or burned
  - Hand clearing is laborious, labor intensive, and slow
- Length of effectiveness/retreatment intervals:
  - Thinning treatments remain effective for one to several years.

Roller chopping operation. (photo by Jeffrey J. Witcosky, U.S. Forest Service)

Roller chopping—Roller chopping is a site preparation technique in which slash and brush are broken into smaller pieces and flattened. In pine flatwoods, the technique is often used to thin out palmettos and is reported to be most effective at reducing palmetto cover when palmettos are wet and already stressed. The technique is also effective at treating thickly vegetated edges and the edge hedge (an edge effect created by prescribed fire ignition techniques). This mechanical method is not recommended for pine rockland habitats.

- Pros:
    - Can widen the burn window
    - Can reduce flame length
    - Considered a good first treatment in an area infrequently burned, such as many newly acquired properties
    - Widely available
    - Feasible method for the WUI area

- Cons:
    - Causes soil disturbance and ground compression (this can be minimized by not double chopping and using lighter equipment)
    - Wheeled prime movers create ruts in soil; this can be minimized by using a tracked vehicle
    - Kills herpetofauna such as gopher tortoises (one way to avoid this is to use flags identifying animal burrows)
    - Roller chopping should not be done in rockland habitat, because the machinery will cause long-lasting damage to the limestone substrate.

- Length of effectiveness/retreatment intervals:
    - Usually used once followed by reintroduction of fire
    - If fire cannot be reintroduced to treatment area, the area will need to be retreated with the roller chopping technique every 3 to 5 years.

Debris from mastication treatment. (photo by Chris Schnepf, University of Idaho)

Mastication—Mastication changes the structure and size of fuels in the stand. Trees and understory vegetation are chopped, ground, or chipped, and the resulting material is usually left on the soil surface. This treatment can be done any time of year, and is used to prepare a site before a burn, to create road access, to remove exotic plants, and to remove oak domes.

- Pros:
  - Can be used in sensitive areas and causes less ground disturbance than chopping
  - Can be used in areas with herpetofauna (populations of reptiles and amphibians)
  - Creates immediate results

- Cons:
  - If masticated fuel is allowed to accumulate, it can create a duff layer that could create smoke and smoldering problems during intense or backing fires. One way to reduce smoldering issues is to burn before the chips dry out.
  - Ground and chopped material covers up mineral soil and rare plants.

- Many problematic species adapted to disturbance quickly resprout following treatment.
  - For larger machines, mastication is typically inefficient at fuel loads of 25 tons per acre or greater.
  - In rockland habitat, some managers reported that metal tracked vehicles cause damage to the substrate; this can be minimized by using a vehicle with flexible tracks.

- Length of effectiveness/retreatment intervals:
  - This method is often a pretreatment to fire. If fire cannot be used in treatment area, the area will need to be retreated with the mastication method every 4 to 5 years.

Mowing—A mower is a device for cutting plants that grow on the ground and is applied to such fuels as grass, shrubs, and palmettos. This method is used in areas around power lines and in the perimeter zones to reduce the edge hedge. It can also be used to mow lines for strip fires and to create escape routes.

- Pros:
  - This method is a less soil-disturbing mechanical option.
  - Assists edges to carry fire by creating fine dead fuels and by opening up unit edges to better airflow
  - Can be used in WUI settings

- Cons:
  - Retreatment frequency is high

- Length of effectiveness/retreatment intervals:
  - Can range from 6 months to 2 years, depending on the treated area

Understory Biomass Reduction Methods

For further information on a variety of mechanical methods and machinery, see these reports:

Windell, Keith; Bradshaw, Sunni. 2000. Understory biomass reduction methods and equipment catalog. Tech. Rep. 0051–2826–MTDC. Missoula, MT: U.S. Department of Agriculture Forest Service, Missoula Technology and Development Center. 156 p. Also available online at: http://www.fs.fed.us/forestmanagement/WoodyBiomassUtilization/tools/mtdc-catalog/index.shtml.

Beckley, B.; Windell, K. 1999. Small-area forestry equipment. Tech. Rep. 9924–2820–MTDC. Missoula, MT: U.S. Department of Agriculture Forest Service, Missoula

Technology and Development Center. 40 electronic p. Also available online at: http://www.fs.fed.us/eng/pubs/pdfpubs/pdf99242820/pdf99242820pt01.pdf.

Guidelines of Use for Mechanical Treatments

The prime mover—The means of moving a treatment device around is called the "prime mover." The prime mover can be an integral part of the device, a tractor, or a bulldozer that pushes or pulls the device as an attachment. Some dedicated devices can have other uses; for instance, a machine with integral chopping head also can be used to pull a plow or disk to maintain fire lines. In general, when considering options for a prime mover, the manager should strive to minimize soil compaction and rutting. Soil compaction is a function of how a machine's weight is distributed to the ground (ground pressure). The ground pressure of wheeled vehicles is usually greater than tracked vehicles. Tracked vehicles spread the weight over a larger surface, resulting in less compaction. However, in pine rocklands, managers have observed that metal-tracked vehicles crush and break up the limestone more than wheeled or rubber-tracked machines. As horsepower increases, so does weight. Consider your horsepower needs carefully. A heavy machine is also more difficult and costly to transport from site to site. Other considerations are listed below.

Checklist for thinking about a mechanical treatment:

- Prime mover
  - Wheeled or tracked
  - Metal or rubber track
  - Dedicated equipment or attachment
  - Cost
  - Power
  - Maintenance needs
  - Reliability
  - Turning radius
  - Weight
  - Transportation among sites
- Safety
  - Operator protection adequate
    - Protection from falling trees/limbs
    - Protection from thrown objects

- Cutter
  - How far do thrown objects travel?
  - Treatment swath width
  - Boom mounted or fixed
    - Boom reach and swing
  - Tooth style:
    - Fixed, hammer or chain flail
  - Vertical or horizontal shaft

Safety/qualifications of operator—Only properly licensed and trained personnel may operate heavy equipment. Other workers in the area of mechanical operations must be constantly vigilant and never approach heavy equipment unless they are certain the operator knows where they are, what they intend to do, and where they intend to go. Personal protective equipment (PPE) should be worn, e.g., hard hats and effective eye protection. Please refer to your agency's policy on PPE.

Safety zones need to be set up prior to operations, taking into consideration throwback distances. Sites should be cleared of barbed wire and other obstacles to avoid machinery damage. Extra consideration needs to be taken in WUI areas.

Communicating with the operator—Often, mechanical treatments are contracted services. The contracted operator may have different experiences or goals about treating an area than those of the land manager. Therefore, the operator must have a clear understanding of the land use objectives of the treatment, the location of sensitive vegetation and any other ecological concerns, and the property boundaries. Several interviewed managers indicated the critical nature of communication and the disastrous results of miscommunication or lack of supervision.

Potential Issues with Mechanical Treatments

Breakdowns—Damaged hydraulic lines are a common source of breakdowns. In the event of hydraulic fluid spills, all machines should have a spill containment kit. Simple techniques can reduce machine damage and downtime. Avoiding hydraulic hose damage can be as simple as never driving "against the grain," especially with roller choppers. When the brush is knocked down during the first pass, the second pass should be taken in the same direction to prevent the flattened vegetation from snagging lines or, more important, injuring the operator.

Treatment site ecology—Mechanical treatments can have a high impact on the site selected for treatment through effects on soils and the rock substrate. Before selecting this type of fuel treatment method, all potential impacts should be considered as well as ways to minimize these impacts.

Disturbing soils—The heavy machinery used in mechanical treatments has the potential to create compacted soils and other disturbances such as ruts. Some ways to minimize soil disturbance include applying treatments when soils are dry, matching the size of the equipment to the size and type of targeted vegetation, and treating targeted areas in one pass. Type of tread is another factor to consider; although tracked vehicles are heavy, they have low ground pressure due to their wide treads.

Invasive species—Soil disturbances create avenues for invasions of exotic and weed species. Actions should be taken to reduce disturbance in treated areas. Chopping and mowing exotic grasses has the potential to spread seeds; one way to prevent the spread is to time treatments before seeds form. There is also a potential to spread exotic species seeds through machinery by "capturing" seeds in tire or tack treads. To ensure that the equipment is not spreading invasive species, vehicles should be washed before moving to another location.

Residual biomass—Mechanical treatments alter the fuel arrangement but do not remove the fuel. The residual biomass left behind can sometimes cause problems when followed up with a prescribed fire. Chip piles left behind after a treatment can smolder and cause smoke issues, and the residual biomass can create duff that will either not burn or burn too well. Timing is important; if fire is to be applied to a site postmechanical treatment, it should be applied soon after and before the residual fuel dries out.

Residual biomass left after a treatment can impact soil and vegetation. Chipped or shredded biomass covers mineral soils, alters soil properties, has unwanted ecological effects, and could create a smoldering fire hazard. One way to reduce this impact is to collect the residual biomass, either during or after treating the site. Depending on the amount, this biomass could be used as mulch in other areas such as walking paths and landscaped sections. It could also be used in the production of alternative energy, such as ethanol.

To learn more about residual biomass use in alternative energy production in Florida, see this Web site for a list of companies: http://www.dep.state.fl.us/energy/energyact/grants.htm or contact Florida Department of Environmental Protection, Florida Energy Office, 2600 Blair Stone Road M/S #19, Tallahassee, FL 32399–2400, telephone 850–245–8002, e-mail: energy@dep.state.fl.us.

Damage to nontarget vegetation—Many important understory plant species in tropical and subtropical pine forests are perennial and subject to mortality or damage by vehicles. In addition, pine trees can become damaged from contact with the equipment or can receive damage to their root system, so it is best to keep equipment outside the edge of the tree crown.

If operating in an area that is not invaded by exotic plant species, keep in mind that treating the site in a mosaic pattern will leave "islands" for seed source as well as for wildlife use.

Wildlife impacts—Some managers found certain techniques could result in greater mortality to herpetofauna. For instance, roller chopping destroys burrow openings and can kill reptiles. Mortality can be reduced by marking burrow openings prior to treatment in order to avoid them.

Operator error—It is important to ensure the operator understands sensitive resources and the objectives of the treatment. Using an experienced operator, providing adequate supervision, and having good communication can reduce operator mistakes.

Public Perceptions of Mechanical Fuel Treatments

A postmechanical treatment site can leave a "mowing down the woods" impression. While the public may not approve of the short-term appearance of the site, having informational brochures available or interpretive signs at the site can help educate the public about the importance of dealing with hazardous fuels and can increase understanding of the long-term benefits.

Costs of Mechanical Fuel Treatments

The cost of mechanical treatments can vary depending on the site, equipment used, and whether it is done in-house or contracted. In general, the per-acre cost can range from $100 to $500 per acre.

Regulations on Mechanical Fuel Treatments

Review all Federal, State, local, and agency regulations on mechanical fuel treatments before operations to ensure compliance. For more information on regulations, see this Web site:

http://www.sfrc.ufl.edu/Extension/florida_forestry_information/planning_and_assistance/environmental_regulations.html or contact your local Florida DOF office at www.fl-dof.com, telephone 850–488–4274.

Section IV: Chemical Fuel Treatments

Chemical treatments in this guide are defined as using an herbicide to kill or control vegetation. Herbicide treatments are generally more expensive than prescribed fire and can have high impacts on nontarget vegetation. These techniques are most often applied in the WUI, in areas heavily invaded by exotics plant species, or to prepare a long unburned stand for a prescribed fire. The number of manufacturers and types of herbicides available is numerous, and having an understanding of how an herbicide functions and how to properly employ the chemical is crucial when deciding on the type of chemical treatment you select to meet your management objective.

Pesticide Disclaimer Clause: This publication contains pesticide information that is subject to change at any time. This information is provided only as a guide. It is always the pesticide applicator's responsibility, by law, to read and follow all current label directions for the specific pesticide being used; it is also the pesticide applicator's responsibility to follow your agency's policies on pesticide use. No endorsement is intended for products mentioned, nor is criticism meant for products not mentioned. The authors assume no liability resulting from the use of this information.

Best Management Practices for Chemical Fuel Treatments

When choosing an herbicide, it is essential to avoid or minimize negative impacts on nontarget organisms, including the ability of the soil to support desirable vegetation. The environment targeted for treatment must be listed on the herbicide label. The following questions are useful when making a site-specific decision about which herbicide to use.

Is the herbicide:

- Effective against the target species

- Least toxic to humans and other nontarget organisms such as desirable vegetation, animals, and beneficial insects

- One that requires an adjuvant? If so, is the adjuvant safe to use in areas with sensitive organisms such as salamanders and other amphibians?

- Least likely to leach into ground or surface water

- Compatible with vegetation and revegetation programs

- Compatible with other management methods

- Quickly degraded in the soil

- Cost effective

Selecting a Herbicide

Knowing how an herbicide functions can help you select the best herbicide for the species you are targeting.

Mode of Action for Herbicide Treatments

An herbicide is often chosen for its mode of action; some of the most common modes of action include:

- Auxin mimics (2,4–D, clopyralid, picloram, and triclopyr) mimic the plant growth hormone auxin, causing uncontrolled and disorganized growth in susceptible plant species.

- Mitosis inhibitors (fosamine) prevent rebudding in spring and new growth in summer,

- Photosynthesis inhibitors (hexazinone), also known as dormancy enforcers, block specific reactions in photosynthesis leading to cell breakdown.

- Amino acid synthesis inhibitors (glyphosate, imazapyr, and imazapic) prevent the synthesis of amino acids required for construction of proteins.

Herbicide Activity

The activity of an herbicide refers to how the chemical enters the plant. Herbicides are either foliar active, soil active, or both.

- Foliar-active chemicals are absorbed by the plant through its leaves, so the chemicals need enough leaf surface to ensure adequate absorption. In some cases, foliar-active chemicals can be applied directly to the stem.

- Soil-active chemicals are pulled into the plant through its roots as the plant takes up water and transpires.

Herbicide Selectivity

The susceptibility or tolerance of different plants to an herbicide is called herbicide selectivity:

- Nonselective herbicides affect all plant types.

- Selective herbicides only affect one type of plant.

Timing of Herbicide Application

Herbicide timing cannot be described in terms of calendar dates, but instead is described in timing of events. There are two broad categories of application timing:

- Preemergent application means the herbicide is applied to the soil before the plant germinates to disrupt germination or kill the germinating seedling.

- Postemergent application means the herbicide is applied directly to the already established plant or soil.

Guidelines of Use for Herbicide Applications

Listed below are general guidelines of herbicide use. You should always refer to the Federal/State/county/agency guidelines for more complete and current policies and information on herbicide use and applicator certification programs.

Herbicide applicator certification—Anyone who applies restricted-use pesticides to any outdoor area in Florida (that are not associated with buildings or public health pest control) must have a pesticide applicator license issued by the Florida Department of Agriculture and Consumer Services, Bureau of Compliance Monitoring, Pesticide Certification & Licensing Section.

For more information on pesticide applicator certification and licensing, please see http://www.flaes.org/complimonitoring/databasesearch/applcert&licensing.html; or contact the

Pesticide Certification & Licensing Section at 3125 Conner Blvd., Bldg. 8 (L–29), Tallahassee, FL 32399–1650, telephone 850–488–3314.

Personal protective equipment for herbicide application—The health and safety of the applicator are a principal concern. Applicators must wear all protective gear required on the label of the herbicide. Please refer to your agency's policy on herbicide use for specific details on PPE.

For more information on choosing suitable PPE, see: "Pesticide Applicator Update: Choosing Suitable Personal Protective Equipment," IFAS Doc. PI–28, Pesticide Information Office, University of Florida, P.O. Box 110710, Gainesville, FL 32611–0710, telephone 352–392–4721, http://edis.ifas.ufl.edu/pdffiles/PI/PI06100.pdf.

Storage of herbicides—The proper storage of herbicides is essential to their safe use. Never store pesticides near food, feed, seed, or animals. Designate an area where only pesticides are to be stored. This area should be secured with a lock and a sign reading: "Warning. Pesticides. Keep Out." The storage area should be well ventilated, cool, and dry. The floor should be concrete or lined with plastic to prevent leaks from reaching the soil.

Containers must be carefully stored and should be labeled to indicate the following: contents (ratio of herbicide, adjuvant, water, etc.); date mixed; and approximate volume remaining when placed in storage. Each type of herbicide should be grouped separately, i.e., group all glyphosate containers together and group all imazapyr containers together. It is good practice to store containers off the ground on wooden pallets to avoid moisture problems. Keep an up-to-date inventory of all chemicals stored; including the date they were purchased, used, and placed into storage.

The storage area should be organized and clean. Have an absorbent, e.g., cat litter, readily available at the storage site to help clean up any spills as well as a shovel, a broom, heavy plastic garbage bags, and a dustpan. Keep a fire extinguisher in the storage area.

Disposal of herbicides—*Avoid excess*—Excess chemicals and empty containers should be disposed of or stored properly. Avoiding herbicide surplus is the best way to minimize disposal issues. Carefully estimate the amount of herbicide needed to complete the treatment application, and buy and mix only what is needed. Determine the size of the area to be treated, calibrate the application equipment, and fill the spray tank (with only the amount needed for the application).

Disposal of rinse water and excess spray mixture—Apply excess spray mixture and rinse water generated from rinsing empty containers and spray tanks to a site consistent with label instructions and management objective. Plan ahead for the application of rinse water and excess spray material to the treated area.

Disposal of containers—Triple wash or pressure rinse empty containers (jugs, drums, etc.). Puncture the container, after rinsing, to prevent reuse. The empty, rinsed container may be taken to a sanitary landfill if the landfill operator and local regulations allow. Empty, rinsed plastic containers may also be taken to a pesticide container recycling program, if one is locally available.

For more information, contact USAg Recycle through their Web site at www.usagrecycling.com or by calling 800–654–3554.

Herbicide spills—Rules and regulations on pesticide spills vary by State and by county. Before obtaining herbicides, call the Florida Department of Agriculture and Consumer

Services, Division of Agricultural Environmental Services, Pesticide Certification Office, telephone 850–488–3314, for up-to-date information on spills and containment in your region.

Recordkeeping of herbicide use—The records you keep on herbicide use not only are required by the law but also will help you evaluate your management techniques in the following ways:

- Help you tell how well a chemical worked, particularly if you have experimented with different concentrations or used alternative application techniques

- Help you figure out how much herbicide you will need in the future so that you will not have to store or dispose of extra chemicals

- May protect you from legal action if you are accused of improper use

- Provide data to respond to surveys conducted by Federal Agencies and universities and that can impact availability of some pesticides through reregistration

- Can be used to address public concern over pesticide use

- Can save money by helping determine the best pesticide management program

For a PDF copy of the Florida Department of Agriculture and Consumer Services' suggested recordkeeping form, see http://www.doacs.state.fl.us/onestop/forms/13340.pdf or contact the Division of Agricultural Environmental Services, 3125 Conner Boulevard, Suite F, Tallahassee, FL 32399–1650, telephone 850–488–3731.

Dyes for herbicides—Incorporating a dye will assist in marking treated plants and areas so that no herbicide is wasted. Some premixed herbicides already contain a dye; others such as the ester-based herbicide Garlon 4® require oil-soluble dyes sold by agricultural chemical and forestry supply companies. Refer to the manufacturer's label for more instructions.

Adjuvants for herbicides—Spray adjuvants (additives) enhance the performance of the herbicide. Adjuvant is a broad term and includes surfactants, oils, antifoaming agents, stickers, and spreaders. It is not always necessary to add an adjuvant.

For more specific information on adjuvants, see, "Spray Additives and Pesticide Formulations." IFAS Factsheet ENH82, February 25, 2003, Florida Cooperative Extension Service, http://edis.ifas.ufl.edu/pdffiles/LH/LH06100.pdf.

Herbicide Application Methods

Foliar treatment—Foliar treatment can be the most cost-effective method of herbicide treatments. These methods apply herbicide directly to the leaves and stems of target plants. All foliar treatments should be made after full leaf expansion in the spring and before fall colors are visible. Allow herbicide treatments to dry for at least 3 hours to allow for adequate absorption.

An adjuvant may be needed to help the herbicide penetrate the plant cuticle—a thick, waxy layer present on leaves and stems of most plants. Refer to the manufacturer's label for more information.

Foliar treatments may be applied by spot spraying, wick, or boom, as described below.

Spot spraying—Rates of 1 gallon or less per minute at low pressure are recommended. Sprayer should be equipped with a flat spray tip or adjustable cone nozzle. Apply herbicide to the leaves and stems of target plants using a consistent back and forth motion. Herbicide should thoroughly coat foliage but not to the point of running off. Complete foliar coverage is needed to be effective. Applications made while walking backward will reduce the risk of the herbicide wicking onto the applicator's clothing.

Wick application—Wick application is recommended where spot spraying is not feasible due to a high concentration of nontarget plants. The wick applicator works by becoming saturated with chemical and is then brushed against the target species. Use of a wick eliminates the possibility of spray drift or droplets falling on nontarget plants.

Boom application—A long horizontal tube with multiple spray heads is mounted or attached to a tractor, all-terrain vehicle, helicopter, or small plane. It is carried above the target area while spraying herbicide, allowing large areas to be treated quickly. Nontarget areas may be affected by this method from movement of the herbicide by vaporization or drift.

Basal sprays—Used for treatment of woody vines, shrubs, and trees. This method applies a band of herbicide penetrant mixture to the lower 12 to 20 inches of the target stem. The herbicide can be applied with a backpack sprayer or a wick. Ester formulations are usually best for basal bark treatments since esters can pass readily through the bark, but you should avoid applying on hot days to prevent vapor drift. Treatment can be performed any time of year; in summer, treatment is best carried out in the mornings when it is cooler. Basal sprays work best on young stems with smooth bark but will not work on older trees with thick bark.

Aerial herbicide application. (photo by U.S. Department of Agriculture, Agricultural Research Service)

Cut-surface (-stump) treatments—Used for treatment of woody species. Herbicide concentrates or mixtures are applied to a freshly cut stem or stump. All cuts should be level, smooth, and free of debris. Herbicide must be applied as quickly as possible after cutting, as a delayed application may reduce the effectiveness of the herbicide. Treatment is most effective in late winter and summer. This method minimizes nontarget damage.

Stem injection treatment—Used for treatment of woody species with large, thick trunks. Herbicide concentrates or mixtures are applied downwards into cuts made around the circumference of the stem. Treatment is most effective in late winter and in summer. Avoid using injection during the spring when sap flow is heavy and can wash out the

herbicide from the cuts. Delay treatment if rainfall is predicted within 48 hours. Herbicides with soil activity can potentially damage nearby nontarget plants if washed out from cuts.

Key Issues Associated with Chemical Treatments

Chemical treatments, while effective, require the fire manager to consider several key issues, including possible ecological impacts, the potential of increasing hazardous fuel risks, and the chance of damage to nontarget plants.

Ecological impacts—Herbicides target biological pathways that are unique only to plants (see "Mode of Action for Herbicide Treatments" above). Most modern herbicides such as glyphosate, imazapyr, and hexazinone degrade quickly, do not persist in the environment, and do not bioaccumulate. When choosing a particular herbicide, be mindful of its mode of action; its environmental fate; and its other characteristics as well as the target site conditions (proximity to water, water table depth, and rare species); target species; and your management objective.

Some herbicide formulations cannot be used in or near water due to toxicity to fish and other organisms. For example, ester formulations are toxic to fish because of the irritation the formulations cause to the gill surfaces. Certain premixed formulations of glyphosate are toxic to aquatic organisms due to the adjuvant it contains. Hexazinone is recognized to be toxic to algae. You can prevent misuse and unintentional consequences by reading the herbicide label and following instructions regarding use in habitats.

The best way to minimize unintended ecological impacts of herbicide use is to select herbicides that are effective against the targeted hazardous fuel, will not move offsite by air or water, are nontoxic to people and wildlife, and will not persist in the environment. However, in some circumstances, a single application of a more toxic or persistent chemical may be preferable. For example, instead of repeated applications of a safer product, a more toxic herbicide will require only a single application. Land managers must strike a balance between the strength or effectiveness of the product and the total negative impact on the environment. The information for making these decisions comes from the herbicide labeling, experienced land managers, herbicide dealers, and other experts.

Adjuvants, additives to herbicides that enhance their performance, do not undergo the same rigorous testing that herbicides do and are not subject to the same restrictions. Some adjuvants can be toxic to fish, shellfish,

Worker using backpack sprayer. (photo by U.S. Forest Service)

and other aquatic invertebrates. It is important to read the manufacturer's label and decide if the formula you choose (whether it contains an adjuvant or if it requires one) will be the best product for your target site and management goals. The herbicide label or Material Safety Data Sheet will specify the best type of adjuvant for the herbicide.

For more information, please see the following resources:

- Chemical Labels and Material Safety Data Sheets are available for free at Crop Data Management Systems' Web site: http://www.cdms.net.

- For help understanding Material Safety Data Sheet language, go to http://edis.ifas.ufl.edu/PI072.

- Environmental fate, toxicology, and other information on specific chemicals can be found at http://extoxnet. orst.edu/.

Increasing hazardous fuel risks—Employing a chemical method to reduce fuel levels will often create a short-term hazardous fuel situation. This is due to the treated vegetation becoming dry and extremely flammable for a short time,

but once the vegetation decomposes, it will no longer be a hazardous fuel. Keep this in mind when creating your hazardous fuels management plan.

Damage to nontarget plants—Depending on the application method and type of herbicide used (selective or nonselective) some nontargeted plants can be affected by the treatment. For example, Journey®, a mixture of imazapic and glyphosate, has been known to kill nontargeted pine trees in treated areas. Another example is imazapyr, a nonselective herbicide that can also cause residual damage to pine trees. To minimize damage to nontarget vegetation, use herbicides appropriate for your targeted species, and use application methods that reduce spray drift and chemical movement. In some cases, nontargeted plants may be unavoidably included in an herbicide treatment. For instance, when treating cogongrass, you have to spray all of the grass as well as a 3-foot buffer to treat the rhizomes, and in doing so, you will invariably kill desirable plants. When deciding on the use of herbicides as a best management practice for hazardous fuels, you will need to consider possible damage that may occur to other species and weigh the risks with the ecological benefits.

Worker injecting herbicide. (photo by U.S. Forest Service)

Public Perception of Herbicide Treatment

The general public perception of herbicide use is negative because of the perceived environmental fate of herbicides and direct toxicity to wildlife. To dispel myths and alleviate concerns, land mangers should educate the public on the benefits of herbicide applications and on the precautions taken for their safe use.

Costs of Herbicide Treatment

Herbicide treatment may be costly due to many factors, including size of treated area, method of application, cost of chemicals, cost of personnel, and cost of retreatments. Typical herbicide costs are $45 to $150 per gallon of herbicide, and treatment costs are $70 to $150 per acre.

Regulations on Herbicide Treatment

Because State and local regulations on herbicide use may be more restrictive than Federal regulations, always check and comply with all State and local regulations. Before developing or implementing any plans for herbicide application, check annual updates from State regulatory and environmental agencies for changes in label restrictions and application policies or permit requirements.

For information of State regulations, visit the Florida Department of Agriculture and Consumer Services's Web site: http://www.doacs.state.fl.us/onestop/aes/registration. html; or check with the Florida Department of Agriculture and Consumer Services, Division of Agricultural Environmental Services, Bureau of Compliance Monitoring at http://www.safepesticideuse.com/.

Additional Information on Herbicide Treatment

Florida Department of Agriculture and Consumer Services
Division of Agricultural Environmental Services
Bureau of Pesticides
3125 Conner Boulevard
Building #6, Mail Stop L29
Tallahassee, FL 32399–1650
Telephone: 850–487–0532
http://www.flaes.org/pesticide/index.html

Table 3 lists common herbicides used in treating hazardous fuels.

Table 3—Common herbicides used in treating hazardous fuels

Herbicide	Brand names	Target	Activity	Example prices (Y2007)	Timing	Notes
Glyphosate	RoundUp®, Rodeo®, and Accord®	Annual and perennial weeds	Foliar	$62 per gallon RoundUp®	Most effective from late summer through fall, but before significant leaf coloring and drop	• Nonselective • Little to no soil activity: binds tightly to soils and is not persistent • Product has desirable traits regarding environmental effects, but some formulations that are premixed with an adjuvant are highly toxic to aquatic organisms
Hexazinone	Velpar® and Pronone®	Annual, biennials, perennial weeds	Soil and some contact foliar activity	$70 per gallon Velpar®	Early spring to early summer when rainfall necessary for activation is available	• Nonselective • Rainfall is necessary for activation • Potential for ground water contamination • Toxic to algae
Imazapic	Plateau®, Plateau Eco-Pak®, and Cadre®	Annual and perennial broadleaf weeds and grasses	Foliar and soil	$266 per gallon Plateau®	Late fall, early spring	• Selective herbicide for both the pre- and postemergent control of some annual and perennial grasses and some broadleaf
Imazapyr	Arsenal®	Annual and perennial grasses, broadleaves, vines, brambles, brush, and trees	Foliar and soil	$312 per gallon Arsenal®	Any time during the growing season from full foliar development	• Nonselective • Provides long-term total vegetation control • Arsenal can cause residual damage to pines
Triclopyr	Garlon® and Remedy®	Woody and annual broadleaf weeds	Foliar with limited soil activity	$91 per gallon Garlon®3A; $120 per gallon Garlon® 4	Garlon® 4 is more effective on woody flatwoods species from midsummer to fall Injection with Garlon® 3A can be effective throughout the year except during periods of heavy sap flow in the spring	• Selective • The ester formulation is highly toxic to aquatic organisms
Isoxaben	Gallery®	Broadleaf weeds	Foliar and soil	$200 per pound Gallery®	Late fall, early spring	• Selective preemergent
Oryzalin	Surflan®	Annual grasses and broadleaf weeds	Soil	$126 per gallon Surflan®	Late fall, early spring	• Selective • Should be applied as a preemergence spray to the soil surface
Fluroxypyr	Vista®	Annual and perennial broadleaf and woody brush	Foliar	$95 per gallon Vista®	Spring to early summer	• Selective • Postemergence • Improves control on hard to control species when used in combination with Garlon® and Tordon® herbicides

Capra hircus *adults.* (photo courtesy of University of Georgia)

Section V: Grazing Fuel Treatment

One management option for reducing hazardous fuels is to utilize livestock to decrease some kinds of surface fuels. This type of treatment involves fencing off selected areas and allowing livestock such as cows or sheep to forage. This technique is most often applied to WUI sites, roadsides, and firebreaks.

Best Management Practices for Grazing Treatments

Grazing converts bulk live fuels to organic waste. Targeted grazing can reduce fuel loads of grasses and shrubs. Managers who utilize grazing on areas with hazardous fuel indicated they use cattle to reduce fine fuels such as grass, sheep to reduce saw palmetto, and goats to reduce ladder fuels such as vines.

Selecting a Grazing Treatment Method

There are several livestock options available. In Florida, most managers reported using cattle, goats, and sheep for grazing.

Targeted grazing reduces grasses and other herbaceous fuels but does not reduce pine needles and deadwood such as branches and logs. Grazing will not reduce all hazardous fuels in a treated area due to the livestock's palette. For instance, sheep will consume grasses and palmetto but not consume gallberry. The fuel reduction achieved by grazing is short term because plants will resprout following grazing. Grazing is most effective when used in maintaining fuel breaks and where prescribed burns are not possible.

- Pros:
  - Can be low cost and even create revenue
  - Minimal labor needed if water and fencing are in place
- Cons:
  - Can compact soils
  - Only affects small diameter (< 3 inches) vegetation
  - Does not reduce dead fuels
  - Fencing and water needed
- Length of effectiveness/retreatment intervals:
  - It is necessary to repeat every 1 to 3 years

Guidelines of Use for Grazing Treatments

Criteria for livestock selection—Each species of grazing animal has different foraging preferences. Cattle prefer grasses but can consume herbaceous forbs and browse in small amounts. Sheep prefer grasses and forbs, and generally do not eat woody plants. Goats prefer woody plants and shrubs over grasses and forbs. To make the most use of targeted grazing, it is important to match the appropriate livestock to the fuel type you are targeting. When selecting a particular livestock, it is important to consider the breed. Given Florida's climate, choose breeds that can withstand heat. For instance, hair sheep are a good choice because of their heat tolerance and parasite resistance. Make sure to discuss the environmental conditions when working with a livestock contractor so that you select the most appropriate breed of livestock for the job.

Stocking rates—To maximize the amount of fuel consumed by livestock, intensive grazing techniques are often used. This involves using a heavy stocking rate for a short period of time in a multiweek rotational cycle. An example would be to use sheep at a stocking rate of 200 animals per acre for 2 to 4 days. Stocking rates and rotations would vary by livestock used, and should be discussed with the contracting grazing company. In a study using goats to reduce hazardous fuels, researchers found that a stocking rate of 600 goats/ha for 1 day significantly reduced fuels. In the same study, researchers used targeted grazing on a fuel break at a stocking rate of 280 goats/ha for 3 days, which significantly reduced cover and biomass.

For more information on grazing for vegetation management, see this online handbook, "Targeted Grazing: A Natural Approach to Vegetation Management and Landscape Enhancement," www.cnr.uidaho.edu/rx%2Dgrazing/Handbook.htm.

Ecological Issues Associated with Grazing Treatments

Targeted grazing in general has low impact on treatment sites. While the impact may be low, before selecting this type of fuel treatment method, all potential impacts should

Cattle grazing in flatwoods. (photo by U.S. Forest Service)

Goat eating saw palmetto. (photo by Karl Schatz, yearofthegoat.net)

be considered, including spread of invasive species, damage to nontarget plants, and endangerment of wildlife.

Invasive species—Livestock can transport invasive plant seeds in their coat and through their waste. Some managers reported exotic plants could be spread through the supplemental feed that is often supplied for the livestock. This can be minimized by using pellet food instead of feed or by providing no supplemental food at all if possible.

Damage to nontarget vegetation—Some nontarget tree species may be affected by grazing. Some may be girdled and killed by livestock eating bark. In general, there is minimal impact on nontarget trees and groundcover.

Wildlife impacts—Where livestock and wildlife interface, there is a potential for disease transmission through contamination of feed and water sources, parasites such as ticks, and insects such as mosquitoes.

Public Perceptions of Fuel Treatments

There is strong public approval for using livestock to reduce hazardous fuel. One example of public support is an experiment using grazing to construct fuel breaks in Carson City, NV. Through a program called "Only Ewes Can Prevent Wildfire," a fenced corridor around Carson City was grazed by ewes (female sheep) and removed

71 to 83 percent of fine fuels. A survey of nearby homeowners revealed that over 90 percent supported the project; most of those polled said they preferred the use of sheep to traditional chemical or mechanical methods of creating fuel breaks.

Costs of Grazing Treatments

The cost to rent livestock varies by area and type of animal used. In some cases, you can generate revenue by leasing areas for livestock such as cattle.

The cost for purchasing your own herd is about $200 to $500 per head, not including costs of maintenance, fencing, and other needs. These costs can be offset by revenue gained from selling the livestock.

Regulations on Grazing Treatments

Review all Federal, State, local, and agency regulations on grazing before beginning this type of treatment.

For more information on regulations, see Web site: http://www.sfrc.ufl.edu/Extension/florida_forestry_information/planning_and_assistance/environmental_regulations.html or contact your local Florida DOF office at www.fl-dof.com, telephone 850–488–4274.

Section VI: Integrated Treatments for Invasive Plant Hazardous Fuels

Controlling invasive plants in pine rocklands and pine flatwoods is critical for reducing wildfire fire risk and preserving the health of native ecosystems. This section covers in detail how to treat six plant species considered both an invasive species and a hazardous fuel. Treating these types of fuels often involves employing a variety of methods such as prescribed fire, and mechanical and chemical treatments.

Old World Climbing Fern (*Lygodium microphyllum*)

Old World climbing fern (*Lygodium*) is a nonnative invasive fern that climbs high into the tree canopy. It also produces a mat of old fern material on the ground that can grow as thick as 3 feet (0.9 m). *Lygodium* reproduces by windblown spores produced throughout the year. A single leaflet can contain up to 28,600 spores.

Identification—Climbing fern is evergreen with dark brown, wiry rhizomes. Fronds climb, twine, and grow up to 90 feet (30 m) long. Main rachis is wiry and stemlike. Leaflets can be fertile or sterile with leafy branches off main rachis that are once-compound and oblong.

Fire effects—*Lygodium* is a concern in management of both wildfire and prescribed burns. In a fire, the fern becomes a ladder fuel, creating flaming mats that carry fire into the canopy, causing intense crown fires. It can carry fire through wet areas that normally are natural barriers to fire and into other fire-sensitive areas through production of flaming brands that ignite spot fires.

What you need to know—When treating this plant, it is easy to unintentionally spread its spores. Physically removing or disturbing this fern can cause spores to spread. Equipment and clothing exposed to this plant can also spread spores to other sites. It is important to wash equipment and clothing before moving them to another site.

The type of herbicide you use will depend on the type of site. For aquatic sites, only herbicides labeled for aquatic use

Lygodium *spp.* (photo courtesy of South Florida Water Management District)

can be applied to or above water. Other herbicides can be applied to sites that are seasonally flooded as long as the site does not contain water at the time of application.

Treatment options—*Ground treatments*—When conducted properly, ground treatments are the most effective way to treat *Lygodium*; unfortunately, depending on the site and degree of the infestation, it may not be the most cost effective or logistically practical. Ground treatments with backpack and handheld sprayers are more selective and can limit damage to nontargeted plants.

A preferred treatment method for ferns that extend high into the canopy is to cut the fern at or below waist height, leaving the clinging portion in the canopy and treating the rooted potion with an herbicide application. This limits disturbance and spread of spores. Fronds that can be reached by handheld sprayer may be left intact.

Herbicides for ground treatments are:

- Glyphosate: rates of 1 to 3 percent of product (4 pounds per gallon) per gallon of water. Note: This is a broad spectrum herbicide that will damage nontarget plants that it comes in contact with.

- Metsulfuron-methyl: rates of 0.02 to 0.04 ounces of product per gallon of water. Note: Use of this herbicide results in less damage to nontargeted plants, but can also result in less control of *Lygodium*.

Due to this plant's tendency to become resistant to a frequently used herbicide, it may be advantageous to experiment with other herbicides.

Aerial spraying—Aerial spraying is nonselective and can cause damage to canopy trees and other vegetation. One way to minimize damage is to conduct aerial spraying during winter months when many nontarget plants may be dormant. Herbicides for aerial spraying are:

- Glyphosate: rates of 7.5 pints of product per acre with a surfactant appropriate for site location (check label for instructions). Note: This is a broad spectrum herbicide that will damage nontarget plants that it comes into contact with.

- Metsulfuron-methyl: rates of 0.05 to 2.0 ounces of product per acre with a surfactant appropriate for site location (check label for instructions). Note: Use of this herbicide results in less damage to nontargeted plants, but can also result in less control of *Lygodium*.

Treating Lygodium *with backpack sprayer.* (photo courtesy of South Florida Water Management District)

Followup treatment—Constant surveillance is needed to detect new infestations and monitor treated areas. Treated sites will need to be retreated 1 to 2 times per year for multiple years. New infestations require immediate response.

Additional information on treating Old World climbing fern—For more information on ongoing experiments with different treatments, visit the Florida Exotic Pest Plant Council Web site to access the current *Lygodium* Management Plan: http://www.fleppc.org/publications.htm.

Downy Rosemyrtle (*Rhodomyrtus tomentosa*)

Downy rosemyrtle is a fast-growing evergreen shrub that forms a dense growth of bushes and can grow to 6 feet (1.8 m) tall. It converts a forested understory into a monocultural thicket.

Downy rosemyrtle produces numerous seeds and a high germination rate. Seeds are dispersed by birds and mammals that eat its fruit.

Identification—This species occurs as small shrubs or trees that can grow to 6 feet (1.8 m) tall. Leaves are opposite, simple, entire, elliptic-ovate, and glossy green above, densely hairy below. Flowers are rose pink in color, 1 inch (2.5 cm) across, with five petals. Fruit is a dark purple berry with aromatic flesh.

Fire effects—This plant is fire adapted and will resprout abundantly after a fire. It is an emerging problem and thought to have the potential to alter fire regimes.

What you need to know—Downy rosemyrtle has proven tolerant of triclopyr herbicide applied by conventional spraying applications. Below are listed methods that have proven effective. The herbicide tebuthiuron is ineffective at controlling downy rosemyrtle.

Flatwoods infested with downy rosemyrtle. (photo by Galileo Group Inc.)

Treatment options—*Chemical control*—Triclopyr (ester formulation) best methods:

Drizzle foliar application in water or oil surfactant at rates of 1 quart per acre. Low volume basal bark application (10 to 20 percent) in oil surfactant applied to at least two opposite sides of the main stem. A repeat application is required. Low output equipment must be used to avoid overdosing.

***Physical control*—**If there are small seedlings or small plants, they can be pulled or dug out by hand. Plants and fruits should be disposed of properly so that they will not be further spread or become dispersed.

***Followup treatment*—**Downy rosemyrtle is an emerging problem. Constant surveillance is needed to detect new infestations and monitor treated areas. Retreatment intervals have not yet been established. New infestations require immediate response to contain them.

Additional information on treating downy rosemyrtle—University of Florida, Institute of Food and Agricultural Sciences Extension Office (IFAS): http://edis.ifas.ufl.edu/index.html.

Melaleuca (*Melaleuca quinquenervia*)

Introduced into south Florida in the 1900s, melaleuca has become one of the most invasive nonnative tree species. This tree grows in dense impenetrable thickets and is highly adapted to fire. Fire facilitates the spread of melaleuca through a massive release of stored seeds. Other disturbance events such as girdling, herbicide application, or stem damage also trigger seed release.

Trees will readily resprout from any point on the bole not killed by fire. They also will resprout from cut stumps. Melaleuca can generate adventitious buds on roots, and broken branches may also root and grow in suitable soil.

Identification—Mature plants are large evergreen trees up to 108 feet (33 m) tall. Trees are slender and branched with drooping irregular branches. Bark is thick and spongy with papery layers and can range in color from whitish to pale cinnamon. Leaves are dull green, simple, elliptic, and densely covered with small hairs when new but becoming smooth with age. Flowers are crowed in spikes, giving a "bottle brush" appearance. Fruits are square woody capsules 0.1 to 0.2 inches (3 to 5 cm) long; each capsule contains up to 300 tiny brown seeds, and a single tree can store as many as 50 million seeds.

Fire effects—The thick, papery bark of melaleuca insulates the living tissue of the tree from fire damage while

Melaleuca fruits and flowers. (photo courtesy of U.S. Geological Survey)

simultaneously carrying the fire into the canopy. Melaleuca leaves contain volatile oils that can create intense crown fires and produce thick, black smoke. Leaf litter created by melaleuca is slow to decompose and can create heavy fuel loads.

What you need to know—There are many management options available when treating melaleuca. Due to the nature of this species and its response to treatments (disturbance), no one treatment type is effective by itself, necessitating an integrated approach of multiple methods.

Treatment options—Treating areas infested with melaleuca requires an integrated management plan (fig. 5). Some factors to consider when creating a management plan include age and degree of infestation; availability of resources (equipment, people); location of the infested site;

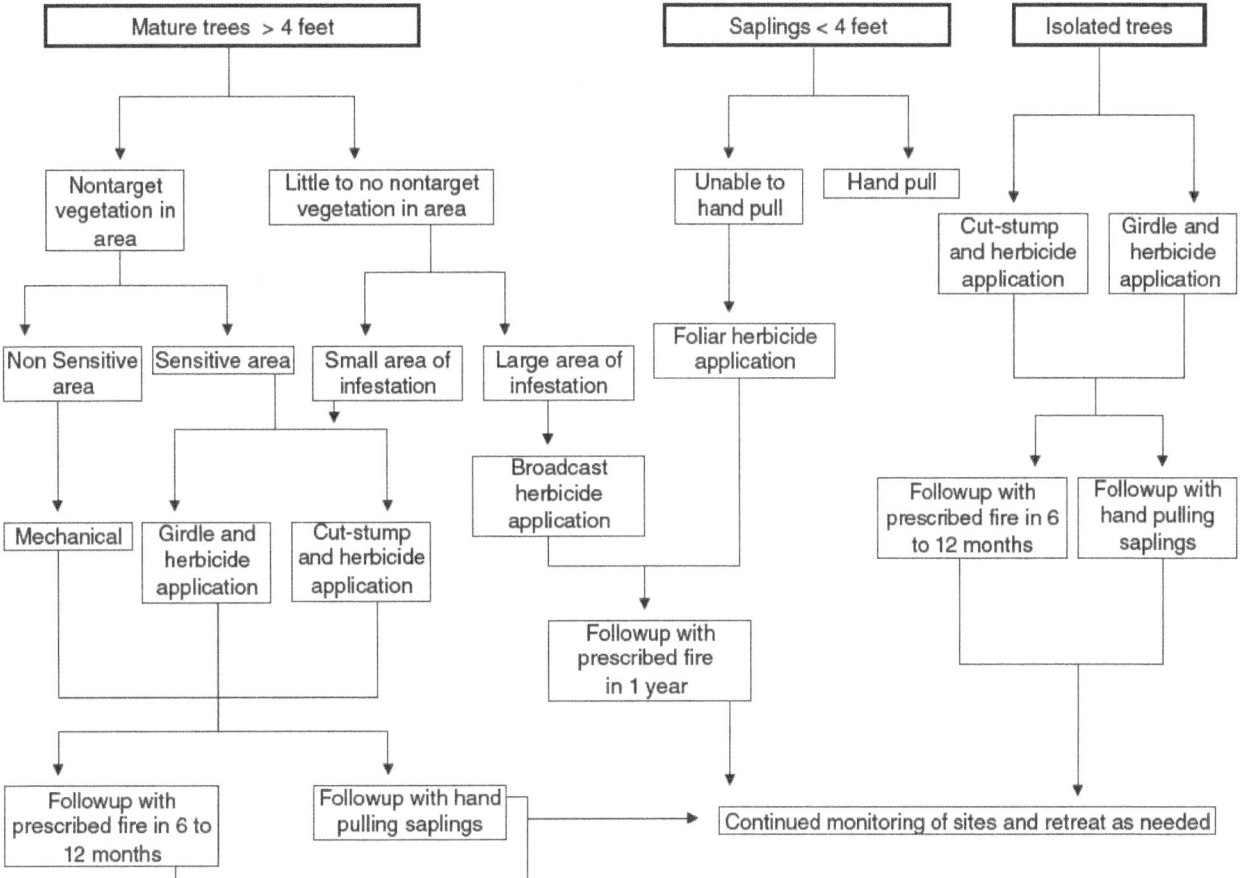

Figure 5—Integrated treatment flowchart for melaleuca control.

and the site's proximity to water. For herbicide applications that require a surfactant, surfactant products that contain methylated seed oil have been shown to be most effective.

Cut stump—These applications are mainly used to treat mature trees > 4 feet (1.2 m) tall. Felling trees will cause an immediate seed release but also will limit the dispersal of seeds by wind. If trees are left onsite, stacking trees limits the sprouting of seedlings to a single area. Before applying an herbicide to a cut stump, make sure that the cut is made as close to the ground as possible to prevent resprouting, and is as level as possible (herbicide will run off of slanted cuts). Remove any sawdust on the stump because sawdust will soak up the herbicide and prevent it from reaching the stump. The herbicide should be applied just inside the bark to the living tissue as soon as possible after the cutting.

Handheld sprayers or squeeze bottles can be used to apply herbicide. Herbicide should be mixed with a dye to keep track of where applications have been made.

Herbicide solutions for cut-stump treatment are:

- Imazapyr: 10 to 25 percent solution of product that contains 2 pounds of imazapyr acid per gallon

- Glyphosate: 50 percent solution or 100 percent of product that contains 3 to 4 pounds of glyphosate acid per gallon

Followup treatment for cut-stump methods are: To remove new seedlings produced from the disturbance created by the cut-stump treatment, site can be burned with a prescribed fire. Wait about 6 to 12 months, after seeds have germinated

Thick smoke from burning melaleuca. (photo courtesy of National Park Service)

but before they have reached a size where they can withstand a fire. Seedlings < 20 inches (< 50 cm) tall can be killed by fire.

Manual methods such as hand pulling may also be used to remove seedlings and saplings that are shorter than 6.5 feet (2 m). This method is laborious and labor intensive and works only in small areas.

Foliar applications—These applications are mainly used for treating saplings that are < 4 feet tall but cannot be pulled out by hand. The applications can also be used for a large area broadcast application where nontarget vegetation does not exist. Be aware that mature trees are difficult to control with foliar applications.

Treat saplings by using a low-volume application with handheld equipment or backpack sprayer and herbicide mixtures that have proven successful:

Glyphosate/imazapyr mixtures diluted in water:

- 5 percent solution of product that contains 3 to 4 pounds of glyphosate acid per gallon and 1-percent solution of product that contains 2 pounds of imazapyr acid per gallon, plus a surfactant (if product does not already contain one)

- 3 percent solution of glyphosate acid and 3 percent solution of imazapyr acid, plus a surfactant (if product does not already contain one)

Glyphosate:

- 5 percent solution of glyphosate acid with surfactant (if product does not already contain one); not as effective as above mixtures; resprouting can occur and more followup treatment will be needed

Herbiciding melaleuca with backpack sprayers. (photo courtesy of National Park Service)

Broadcast applications—For broadcast applications, use glyphosate/imazapyr mixtures. Apply 3 pounds of glyphosate acid per acre and 1.5 pounds of imazapyr per acre, plus surfactant. Apply at a rate of 10 gallons per acre by helicopter, making at least two overlapping passes in opposite directions for a total application rate of 20 gallons per acre. Nozzle sizes 0.020 to 0.030 will provide best coverage.

Some trees treated with herbicide have been observed to resprout after a fire. To ensure maximum success of foliar herbicide treatments, wait at least 1 year after herbicide application before conducting a followup burn.

Girdle applications—This method can be used for isolated trees or for stands where aerial application is not feasible due to location or nontarget plants in the area. Downward cuts are made around the bark using a machete. Cuts should be made deep enough to expose living tissue. An herbicide should then be applied using a handheld sprayer; an adequate amount should be applied to the girdle to make sure the tissue is thoroughly wet.

While this method of herbicide application can be effective at killing melaleuca and minimizing damage to nontarget vegetation, it has drawbacks in efficiency. The method is labor intensive, slow, and costly.

Hack-and-squirt treatment of melaleuca. (photo courtesy of South Florida Water Management District)

Herbicide mixtures for girdle applications:

- Diluted in water: 25 percent glyphosate product that contains 3 to 4 pounds of glyphosate acid per gallon and 25 percent imazapyr product that contains 2 pounds of imazapyr acid per gallon

- Diluted in water: 10 percent imazapyr product that contains 2 pounds of imazapyr acid per gallon and 50 percent glyphosate product diluted in water that contains 3 to 4 pounds of glyphosate acid per gallon

- A solution of 50 to 100 percent glyphosate product that contains 3 to 4 pounds of glyphosate acid per gallon can be used alone but is not as effective as above mixtures. Resprouting can occur, and more followup treatment will be needed.

Followup treatment for girdle applications: To remove new seedlings produced from the disturbance created by girdle application, herbicide treatment can be followed up with a prescribed fire. Wait about 6 to 12 months, after seeds have germinated but before they have reached a size where they can withstand a fire. Seedlings < 20 inches (< 50 cm) tall can be killed by fire.

Manual methods such as hand pulling may also be used to remove seedlings and saplings that are shorter than 6.6 feet (2 m). This method is labor intensive and works only in small areas.

Soil applications—Granular or liquid herbicides can be applied to the soil and are taken up by the roots. They can be applied by helicopter over the tree canopy in large areas of infestation, or on the ground using a specialized blower. Herbicide for soil applications is 4 pounds of hexazinone per acre can be used in either liquid or granular form.

Treatment may need to be followed up to remove new seedlings produced from the disturbance created by herbicide application. Wait about 6 to 12 months, after seeds have germinated but before they have reached a size where they can withstand a fire. Seedlings < 20 inches (< 50 cm) tall can be killed by fire.

Manual methods such as hand pulling may also be used to remove seedlings and saplings that are shorter than 6.6 feet (2 m). This method is labor intensive and works only in small areas.

Mechanical methods—Removing melaleuca with mechanical methods involves using logging or heavy-duty mowing equipment. These methods can be used to treat mature trees. Seedlings, saplings, and remaining stumps will require followup treatment with an herbicide application. Mechanical methods using heavy equipment may not be appropriate for sensitive areas where melaleuca most often occurs because of disturbance from heavy machinery to soil and nontarget vegetation.

Biological control methods—Biological controls involve the use of live natural enemies to control pests. These methods do not eradicate the pest but are intended to reduce the population density below economically or environmentally significant levels. Starting a biological control program requires a consistent commitment of time and money for research. But once the insects have been released and have become established, these methods provide a highly cost-effective tool for suppressing melaleuca, because the insects are cost free (beyond the initial research investment), self sustaining, and self dispersing.

For more about biological controls or to order biological control insects from the University of Florida IFAS, visit Web site: http://kgioeli.ifas.ufl.edu/biocontrolorder.htm or call 772–462–1660.

Additional information on treating melaleuca—For more information on the treatment options listed above for melaleuca, as well as updates on integrated management plan options, demonstration sites, and research, visit The Areawide Management and Evaluation of Melaleuca web site: http://tame.ifas.ufl.edu/. To download a copy of their most recent land manager's handbook, go to http://tame.ifas.ufl.edu/html/documents/LandManagersHandbookNF.pdf.

Cogongrass plume. (photo courtesy of River to River Cooperative Weed Management Area)

Cogongrass (*Imperata cylindrica*)

Cogongrass, one of the most problematic invasive species, is ranked in the top 10 of the worst weeds in the world (Holm and others 1977). It is adapted to disturbance, poor soils, high-light and low-light environments, drought conditions, and fire. In Florida it infests pastures, ditch banks, roadsides, and forests. This grass grows from 2 feet (0.6 m) to over 4 feet (1.2 m) in height, and when burned, creates hot, flashy fires. It can introduce fire into sensitive areas that are not usually burned, and it can change the fire regime of fire-dependant ecosystems by altering the fuel structure of the invaded areas.

Identification—Cogongrass grows as a perennial rhizomatous grass native to Southeast Asia. It grows in loose to compact bunches; each bunch contains several leaves arising from the mid area of the rhizome. Leaves are 1 inch wide, have a prominent offcenter white midrib, and end in a sharp point. Leaf margins are finely serrated and embedded with silica crystals (which deter herbivory). Flowers are arranged in a silvery tube-shaped branching structure 3 to 11 inches (7.6 to 28 cm) long and 1.5 inches (3.8 cm) wide. Seeds with long fluffy white plumes are produced year round but occur predominately in the spring.

Fire effects—Cogongrass creates hot, flashy fires due to greater fine fuel loads and high biomass. In heavy stands of cogongrass, flame lengths can be more than 15 feet (5 m) with extremely rapid rates of spread. These hot fires can kill tree seedlings and juvenile trees.

What you need to know—Cogongrass rhizomes are responsible for the survival and short distance spread of the grass. Cogongrass can quickly recover from cutting and burning because more than 60 percent of the plant's total biomass is found in the rhizomes; in addition, the roots and rhizomes are fire resistant. In established areas, cogongrass produces over 3 tons of rhizomes per acre. The rhizomes are known to produce allopathic chemicals that inhibit the growth of other plant species, and once cogongrass is established, the rhizomes grow so dense that other plant species become excluded and normal ecological succession will not take place.

Treatment options—There are several different methods for treating cogongrass, but no method is effective alone. To effectively control cogongrass, an integrated management approach using multiple methods should be considered (fig. 6).

An integrated management plan involves several steps. Research has shown the most effectives steps are mowing or burning, disking, herbicide, revegetation, and followup herbicide spot treatments. Your integrated management

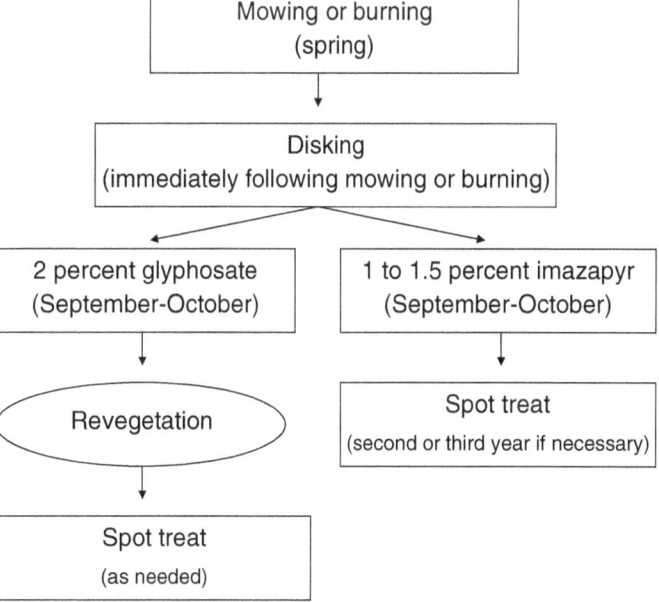

Figure 6—An integrated approach to cogongrass management in the Southeastern United States (Jose and others 2002).

plan should be tailored to your treatment site and take into account such factors as site sensitivity and your long-term management goals. It may not be possible to use all of the methods outlined below, but the most effective control will be achieved by using as many of the steps as possible.

Mowing or burning—This is best done in the spring or summer. It forces rhizomes to produce new shoots and depletes carbohydrate reserves, weakening the rhizomes.

Disking or tilling—After regrowth begins, the treatment area should be disked or tilled as deeply as possible to break up the weakened rhizomes. This treatment may not be applicable to all areas, especially environmentally sensitive areas.

Herbicide—Treatment is best applied in the fall (from September to October) when there has been sufficient regrowth of aboveground shoots. The herbicide application should extend at least 10 feet (3 m) beyond the extent of the infested area. Herbicide trials for treatment of cogongrass have been extensively conducted throughout the world; of all herbicides reviewed, imazapyr and glyphosate are most effective. Your preference of herbicide depends on your treatment plan. If your plan includes immediate revegetation, then a 2-percent solution of glyphosate should

be used because this solution does not have residual soil activity. If no revegetation is planned, a 1- to 1.5-percent solution of imazapyr could be used because this solution has residual soil activity. Keep in mind that, due to its high soil activity, imazapyr can leach into ground water, and that its improper application can damage nearby vegetation.

Revegetation—Introducing desirable vegetation can slow the reinfestation of cogongrass and assist in preventing soil erosion after an herbicide application. Species should be chosen that will compete successfully with cogongrass over the long term.

Followup—Spot treatment using an herbicide may be needed to maintain the treated area. Regular surveillance of treated and untreated areas will assist in determining if cogongrass is present. Identifying the presence of cogongrass and developing an integrated management plan to prevent further spread will assist in achieving greatest control of this invasive grass.

Additional information on treating cogongrass—For up-to-date publications and treatment methods, visit www.cogongrass.org and the Florida DOF Web site, which includes pictures and treatment descriptions: www.fl-dof.com/forest_management/fh_invasives_cogon.html.

Cogongrass infestation in flatwoods. (photo courtesy of River to River Cooperative Weed Management Area)

Burma reed. (photo courtesy of National Park Service)

Burma reed, cane grass, silk reed (*Neyraudia reynaudiana*)

Burma reed (*Neyraudia*) is an extremely invasive, tall cane grass adapted to fire. It invades disturbed sites, dry open habitats, and pine rockland habitat. It prefers dry sites but has been discovered in marshy areas with moist soils. Once established, it will invade undisturbed areas. It alters plant communities by shading out understory plants, and creates conditions that can produce extremely hot, destructive wildfires. In pine rockland habitat, the understory is generally 3.3 to 5 feet (1 to 1.5 m) in height. A *Neyraudia* invasion can raise the understory to 13 to 15 feet (4 to 5 m) in height and increase the fine fuel load by 3 tons per acre.

Identification—*Neyraudia* is a tall perennial plume grass that grows up to 15 feet (5 m) in height. It grows in clumps that each produce 40 stalks and 12 to 20 flowering plumes. Flowering plumes are composed of hundreds of tiny flowers and have a silky appearance. Each plume can be up to 3 feet (1 m) in length. Stems are round, solid, and have nodes every 3 to 5 inches (7.6 to 12.7 cm). Leaves are 8 to 10 inches (20 to 25 cm) long.

Fire damage—*Neyraudia* is adapted to fire and highly combustible, and alters fire regimes by increasing fine fuel biomass. The increase in biomass results in greater fire intensity, higher flame lengths, and increased heat transfer to the canopy, resulting in overstory mortality. The feathery flower plumes carry flames high into the air and can detach, causing spot fires. *Neyraudia's* high flammability promotes frequent fires that enhance the spreading of this invasive grass.

What you need to know—Early detection and aggressive control is the most effective management approach. Areas infested with *Neyraudia* require long-term commitment to ensure successful restoration.

Treatment options—An effective management option involves an integrated approach of cutting, mowing, or burning, with herbicide treatment and revegetation.

Cutting or burning

- Cutting: If treating individual plants, you can hand-cut stalks using a steel blade adaptor for a string trimmer. Remove cut stems and seed heads from site, taking measures to ensure seeds do not become detached.

- Burning: This method will reduce the plant's stalks to ash and eliminate the cost of vegetation removal.

Herbicide—Immediately after cutting, the remaining portions of the grass can be sprayed with 2 to 5 percent glyphosate mixed with an acidic surfactant to prevent new growth. If any further resprouting occurs, the new growth should be treated with a second herbicide application.

After a fire, *Neyraudia* rapidly resprouts. Once the new growth reaches 12 to 18 inches (30 to 46 cm), an herbicide can be applied without concern about nontarget vegetation damage. Foliar application of 2 to 5 percent glyphosate mixed with an acidic surfactant.

Revegetation—Following an herbicide application, introducing desirable vegetation can slow the reinfestation of *Neyraudia*. Species should be chosen that will compete successfully with *Neyraudia* over the long term.

The Plant Conservation Alliance lists several native grasses that can be substituted for *Neyraudia*:

- Fakahatchee grass (*Tripsacum dactyloides*)

- Switchgrass (*Panicum virgatum*)

- Muhly grass (*Muhlenbergia capillaris*)

In the pine rocklands:

- Florida little bluestem (*Schizachyrium rhizomatum*)

- Wire bluestem (*Schizachyrium gracile*)

- Purple three awn (*Aristica purpurea*)

- Florida gamagrass (*Tripsacum floridanum*)

In coastal uplands or disturbed sites:

- Pinewoods fingergrass (*Eustachys petraea*)

Followup—Regular surveillance of treated and untreated areas will assist in determining if *Neyraudia* is present. To maintain the treated area, repeated herbicide treatments may be needed to deal with any new growth that emerges over the next couple of years.

Additional information on treating *Neyraudia*—The Plant Conservation Alliance: http://www.nps.gov/plants/alien/ and The Nature Conservancy's Element Stewardship Abstracts: http://conserveonline.org/docs/2001/05/neyrrey.rtf.

Guineagrass (*Urochloa maxima*) formerly (*Panicum maximum*)

Guineagrass, native to tropical areas in Africa, is considered an important feed crop for livestock in that part of the world. But it is an invasive pest in many tropical areas, including Florida, Australia, and Hawaii. In Florida, it is common in fields, groves, roadsides, and other disturbed sites. It is a drought-resistant grass that quickly builds up a high biomass of plant material. When burned, guineagrass creates hot flashy fires.

Identification—Guineagrass is a tufted perennial that grows 5 to 10 feet (1.5 to 3 m) tall. It usually grows in large bunches from short stout rhizomes. Leaf blades are long, narrow, finely tipped, and 0.4 inches (1 cm) wide with a prominent midrib. Seed heads are branched, and the oblong seeds are white to purple in color.

Fire effects—Guineagrass forms dense stands and generates a high fine fuel load that when burned, creates a dangerous blaze. Guineagrass is adapted to fire and, once burned, will quickly recolonize.

Treatment options

Herbicide—Foliar application of 2 percent glyphosate.

Biological—Plants have been noted to die rapidly under close continuous grazing.

Followup—Regular surveillance of treated and untreated areas will assist in determining if guineagrass is present. To maintain the treated area, repeated herbicide treatments may be needed to deal with any new growth that emerges over the next couple of years.

Guinea grass. (photo courtesy of National Park Service)

References

Adams, S.N. 1975. Sheep and cattle grazing in forests: a review. The Journal of Applied Ecology. 12(1): 143–152.

Beckley, B.; Windell, K. 1999. Small-area forestry equipment. 9924–2820–MTDC. Missoula, MT: U.S. Department of Agriculture Forest Service, Technology and Development Program. 40 electronic p.

Bellinger, R. 2005. Pesticide recordkeeping. http://entweb. clemson.edu/pesticid/saftyed/recordkp.htm#benefits. [Date accessed: November 9, 2006].

Bengis, R.G.; Kock, R.A.; Fischer, J. 2002. Infectious animal diseases: the wildlife/livestock interface. Revue Scientifique et Technique de l'Office International des Epizooties. 21(1): 53–65.

Bennett, M.; Fitzgerald, S. 2006. Reducing hazardous fuels on woodland properties. http://extension.oregonstate.edu/ sorec/Forestry/. [Date accessed: June 2007].

Brockway, D.G.; Outcalt, K.W. 2000. Restoring longleaf pine wiregrass ecosystems: hexazinone application enhances effects of prescribed fire. Forest Ecology and Management. 137(1–3): 121–138.

Brose, P.; Wade, D. 2002a. Potential fire behavior in pine flatwood forests following three different fuel reduction techniques. Forest Ecology and Management. 163(1–3): 71–84.

Brose, P.H.; Wade, D. 2002b. Understory herbicide as a treatment for reducing hazardous fuels and extreme fire behavior in slash pine plantations. In: Outcalt, Kenneth W., ed. Proceedings of the eleventh biennial southern silvicultural research conference. Gen. Tech. Rep. SRS–48. Asheville, NC: U.S. Department of Agriculture Forest Service, Southern Research Station: 109–113.

Calkin, D. 2005. Economic uses fact sheet 9: mechanical treatment costs. RMRS–RN–20–9–WWW. Fort Collins, CO: U.S. Department of Agriculture Forest Service, Rocky Mountain Research Station. 2 p.

Carter-Finn, K.; Hodges, A.; Lee, D.; Olexa, M. 2006a. Management of melaleuca by professional land managers in south Florida. Gainesville, FL: University of Florida, Institute of Food and Agricultural Sciences. 13 p.

Carter-Finn, K.; Hodges, A.; Lee, D.; Olexa, M. 2006b. Management of melaleuca by residents in south Florida. Gainesville, FL: University of Florida, Institute of Food and Agricultural Sciences. 6 p.

Chapman, C.K.; Reid, C.R. 2004. Sheep and goats: ecological tools for the 21st century. Utah State University Extension Electronic Publication. http://extension.usu. edu/files/factsheets/Sheep%20and%20Goats.pdf. [Date accessed: June 14, 2010].

Corbett, J.L.; Askew, S.D.; Thomas, W.E.; Wilcut, J.W. 2004. Weed efficacy evaluations for bromoxynil, glufosinate, glyphosate, pyrithiobac, and sulfosate. Weed Technology. 18(2): 443–453.

Department of Natural Resources and Water. 2006. Guinea grass. www.nrw.qld.gov.au. [Date accessed: March 10, 2007].

Everest, J.; Patterson, M. 1997. Brush control. Publ. ANR–1058. Auburn University, AL: Alabama Cooperative Extension System. 12 p.

Faircloth, W.: Patterson, M.; Miller, J.; Teem, D. 2005. First-year herbicide release options for cogongrass control in loblolly pine plantations. Proceedings of the 58th annual meeting of the Southern Weed Science Society. 58: 245 p.

Ferriter, A.; Serbesoff-King, K.; Bodle, M. [and others]. 2004. Exotic species in the Everglades Protection Area. In: 2004 Everglades consolidated report. West Palm Beach, FL: South Florida Water Management District: 11–15.

Florida Department of Agriculture and Consumer Services. 2006. Suggested pesticide recordkeeping form. http://www.doacs.state.fl.us/onestop/forms/13340.pdf. [Date accessed: January 9, 2007].

Florida Department of Community Affairs. 2004. Wildfire mitigation in Florida. Jacksonville, FL.

Florida Exotic Pest Plant Council. 2006. Old World climbing fern (*Lygodium microphyllum*) management plan for Florida. 2[d] ed. Florida Exotic Pest Plant Council Lygodium Task Force. 109 p.

Florida Fish and Wildlife Conservation Commission. 2004. Florida's endangered species, threatened species and species of special concern. http://myfwc.com/ imperiledspecies/pdf/Endangered-Threatened-Special-Concern-2004.pdf. [Date accessed: October 2007].

Florida Keys Invasive Exotics Task Force. 2005. Florida Keys invasive exotics task force (FKIETF) list of invasive plants of the Florida Keys. http://www.keysgreenthumb. net/exotics_list.pdf. [Date accessed: February 20, 2007].

Fowlkes, M.D.; Michael, J.L.; Crisman, T.L.; Prenger, J.P. 2003. Effects of the herbicide imazapyr on benthic macroinvertebrates in a logged pond cypress dome. Environmental Toxicology and Chemistry. 22(4): 900–907.

Grelen, H.E.; Pearson, H.A.; Thill, R.E. 1985. Response of slash pines to grazing from regeneration to the first pulpwood thinning. In: Shoulders, E., ed. Proceedings of the third biennial southern silvicultural research conference. Gen. Tech. Rep. SO–54. New Orleans: U.S. Department of Agriculture Forest Service, Southern Forest Experiment Station: 523–527.

Guala, G.I. 2005. Element steward abstract: *Neyraudia reynaudiana*. Invasive species initiative. http://tncweeds. ucdavis.edu/esadocs/neyrreyn.html. [Date accessed: February 15, 2007].

Holm, L.G.; Plucknett, D.L.; Pancho, J.V.; Herberger, J.P. 1977. The world's worst weeds: distribution and biology. Honolulu: University Press of Hawaii. 609 p.

Hutchinson, J.; Langeland, K.; Ferriter, A. 2004. Notes from the *Lygodium* research review meeting. Wildland Weeds. 7(4): 6–8.

Invasive Species Specialist Group. 2005. *Neyraudia reynaudiana* (grass). Invasive Species Specialist Group database. www.issg.org/database/species/ecology. [Date accessed: January 8, 2007].

Invasive Species Specialist Group. 2006. Ecology of *Urochloa maxima* (grass). Invasive Species Specialist Group database. http://www.issg.org/. [Date accessed: March 3, 2007].

Johnson, E.; Shilling, D.G. 2005. Fact sheet: cogon grass. www.nps.gov/plants/alien. [Date accessed: February 15, 2007].

Jose, S.; Cox, J.; Miller, D.L. [and others]. 2002. The story of cogongrass in southern forests. Journal of Forestry. 100(1): 41–44.

Kline, W.; Duquesnel, J. 1996. Management of invasive exotic plants with herbicides in Florida. Down to Earth. 51: 22–28.

Langeland, K.; Burks, C. 1998. Identification and biology of non-native plants in Florida's natural areas. Gainesville, FL: University of Florida, Institute of Food and Agricultural Sciences.

Langeland, K.; Meisenburg, M. 2005. Professional applicator's guide to herbicides for melaleuca control. Gainesville, FL: University of Florida, Institute of Food and Agricultural Sciences, Cooperative Extension Service. 4 p.

Langeland, K.A.; Hutchinson, J. 2005. Natural area weeds: Old World climbing fern (*Lygodium microphyllum*). Original publication date: August 2001. Revised: June 2005. UF/IFAS Doc. SS–AGR–21. Gainesville, FL: University of Florida. 4 p.

Langeland, K.A.; Stocker, R.K. 2001. Control of non-native plants in natural areas of Florida. 2^{d} ed. Gainesville, FL: University of Florida, Institute of Food and Agricultural Sciences, Cooperative Extension Service. 31 p.

Lewis, C.E.; Tanner, G.W.; Terry, W.S. 1988. Plant response to pine management and deferred-rotation grazing in north Florida. Journal of Range Management. 41: 460–465.

Lippincott, C.L. 2000. Effects of *Imperata cylindrica* (l.) Beauv. (cogongrass) invasion on fire regime in Florida sandhill (USA). Natural Areas Journal. 20(1): 140–149.

Litt, A.R.; Provencher, L.; Tanner, G.W.; Franz, R. 2001. Herpetofaunal responses to restoration treatments of longleaf pine sandhills in Florida. Restoration Ecology. 9(4): 462–474.

Lopez-Zamora, I.; Comerford, N.B.; Muchovej, R.M. 2004. Root development and competitive ability of the invasive species *Melaleuca quinquenervia* (Cav.) S.T. Blake in the south Florida flatwoods. Plant and Soil. 263(1–2): 239–247.

Lott, M.; Volin, J. 2001. Dispersal, reproduction and physiological ecology of two invasive non-indigenous fern species, *Lygodium microphyllum* and *Lygodium japonicum*. Wildland Weeds. 4(4): 5.

MacDonald, G. 2004. Cogongrass (*Imperata cylindrica*) biology, ecology, and management. Critical Reviews in Plant Science. 23(5): 367–380.

MacDonald, G.; Brecke, B.; Langeland, K. [and others]. 2006. Cogongrass (*Imperata cylindrica* (l.) Beauv.) biology, ecology, and management in Florida. Gainesville, FL: University of Florida, Institute of Food and Agricultural Sciences. 3 p.

Michael, J.L.; Crisman, T.L.; Prenger, J.; Fowlkes, M.D. 1998. Movement of herbicide and nutrients from flatwoods sites into wetlands, and their impacts on wetlands biota. Paper presented at the annual review meeting, National Council for Air and Stream Improvement forested wetlands study. 1997 annual report. Gainesville, FL: University of Florida: 16–19.

Miller, D.A.; Wigley, T.B. 2004. Introduction: herbicides and forest biodiversity. Wildlife Society Bulletin. 32(4): 1016–1019.

Miller, J.H. 2003. Nonnative invasive plants of southern forests: a field guide for identification and control. Gen. Tech. Rep. SRS–62. Asheville, NC: U.S. Department of Agriculture Forest Service, Southern Research Station. 93 p.

Miller, K.V.; Miller, J.H. 2004. Forestry herbicide influences on biodiversity and wildlife habitat in southern forests. Wildlife Society Bulletin. 32(4): 1049–1060.

Motooka, P. 2000. Summaries of herbicide trials for pasture, range, and non-cropland weed control—1999. Honolulu: College of Tropical Agriculture and Human Resources. 7 p.

Motooka, P.; Ching, L.; Nagai, G. 2002. Herbicidal weed control methods for pastures and natural areas of Hawaii. WC–8. Honolulu: Institute of Tropical Agriculture and Human Resources. 35 p.

Myers, R.L.; Belles, H.A.; Snyder, J.R. 2001. Prescribed fire in the management of *Melaleuca quinquenervia* in subtropical Florida. In: Galley, Krista E.M.; Wilson, Tyrone P., eds. Proceedings of the invasive species workshop: the role of fire in the control and spread of invasive species. Misc. Publ. 11. Tallahassee, FL: Tall Timbers Research Station: 132–140.

Neary, D.G.; Michael, J.L. 1985. Herbicides in Florida's flatwoods-efficacy and opportunity. In: Plywell, Nancy A.; Neary, Daniel; Law, Beverly, comps., eds. Herbicides for southern forestry: Proceedings of the 17th annual spring symposium. Gainesville, FL: School of Forest Resources and Conservation; Florida Society of American Foresters: 194–201.

Neary, D.G.; Michael, J.L. 1996. Herbicides—protecting long-term sustainability and water quality in forest ecosystems. New Zealand Journal of Forestry Science. 26(1/2): 241–264.

Nielsen, O.K.; Chikoye, D.; Streibig, J.C. 2005. Efficacy and costs of handheld sprayers in the subhumid savanna for cogongrass control. Weed Technology. 19(3): 568–574.

Olson, B.; Launchbaugh, K. 2006. Managing herbaceous broadleaf weeds with targeted grazing. In: Launchbaugh, K., ed. Targeted grazing: a natural approach to vegetation management and landscape enhancement. Centennial, CO: Cottrell Printing: 57–66.

Page-Dumroese, D. 2005. Environmental consequences fact sheet 14: fuels reduction and compaction. RMRS–RN–23–14–WWW. Moscow, ID: U.S. Department of Agriculture Forest Service, Rocky Mountain Research Station. 2 p.

Pemberton, R.; Ferriter, A. 1998. Old World climbing fern (*Lygodium microphyllum*), a dangerous invasive weed in Florida. American Fern Journal. 88(4): 165–175.

Pittroff, W.; Narvaez, N.; Ingram, R. [and others]. 2006. Prescribed herbivory for fire fuels management. In: Barry, S.; Risberg, D., eds. Grazing for biological conservation: lessons learned from grazing studies. San Jose, CA: University of California Cooperative Extension: 1–2.

Platt, W.; Gottschalk, R. 2001. Effects of exotic grasses on potential fine fuel loads in the groundcover of south Florida slash pine savannas. International Journal of Wildland Fire. 10(2): 155–159.

Platt, W.; Lee, S. 2004. Managing invasions of fire-frequented ecosystems: hardwoods and graminoids in southeastern savannas, prairies, and marshes. Ecological Restoration. 22(4): 304.

Ramsey, C.L.; Jose, S.; Miller, D.L. [and others]. 2003. Cogongrass [*Imperata cylindrica* (L.) Beauv.] response to herbicides and disking on a cutover site and in a mid-rotation pine plantation in Southern USA. Forest Ecology and Management. 179(1–3): 195–207.

Rummer, R. 2004. Economic uses fact sheet 1: mastication treatment and costs. RMRS–RN–20–1–WWW. Moscow, ID: U.S. Department of Agriculture Forest Service, Rocky Mountain Research Station. 2 p.

Serbesoff-King, K. 2003. Melaleuca in Florida: a literature review on the taxonomy, distribution, biology, ecology, economic importance and control measures. Journal of Aquatic Plant Management. 41: 98–112.

Sharma, S.D.; Singh, M. 2000. Optimizing foliar activity of glyphosate on *Bidens frondosa* and *Panicum maximum* with different adjuvant types. Weed Research. 40(6): 523–533.

Shilling, D.G. 1996. Integrated management of cogongrass for native habitat restoration (*Imperata cylindrica*). In: Proceedings of the ecosystem restoration workshop. Lakeland, FL: Florida Institute of Phosphate Research and Society for Ecological Restoration: 21–22.

Stanturf, J.; Rummer, R.; Wimberly, M. [and others]. 2003. Developing an integrated system for mechanical reduction of fuel loads at the wildland/urban interface in the United States. In: Proceedings of the 2d forest engineering conference. Uppsala, Sweden: Skogforsk: 135–138.

Starr, F.; Starr, K.; Loope, L. 2003. A field guide to the early detection of invasive plants and animals on Maui, Hawai'i. Maui, Hawaii: U.S. Geological Survey. 57 p.

Swearingen, J. 2005a. Fact sheet: burma reed. www.nps.gov/plants/alien. [Date accessed: January 12, 2007].

Swearingen, J. 2005b. Fact sheet: paperbark tree. www.nps. gov/plants/alien. [Date accessed: February 4, 2007].

Tatum, V.L. 2004. Toxicity, transport, and fate of forest herbicides. Wildlife Society Bulletin. 32(4): 1042–1048.

Taylor, C.A., Jr. 2006. Targeted grazing to manage fire risk. In: Launchbaugh, K., ed. Targeted grazing: a natural approach to vegetation management and landscape enhancement. Centennial, CO: Cottrell Printing: 107–114.

Texas Agricultural Extension Service. 1999. Herbicides: how they work and the symptoms they cause. http:// lubbock.tamu.edu/focus/Off_Season/FlexCotton/PDF/ Herbicides.pdf. [Date accessed: December 8, 2009].

Thomas, B.J.; Brandt, L. 2003. Monitoring ground treatments of Old World climbing fern (*Lygodium microphyllum*) on the Arthur R. Marshall Loxahatchee NWR. Wildland Weeds. 6(6): 9–11.

Treweek, J.R.; Watt, T.A.; Hambler, C. 1997. Integration of sheep production and nature conservation: experimental management. Journal of Environmental Management. 50(2): 193–210.

Tsiouvaras, C.N.; Havlik, N.A.; Bartolome, J.W. 1989. Effects of goats on understory vegetation and fire hazard reduction in a coastal forest in California. Forest Science. 35(4): 1125–1131.

Tu, M.; Hurd, C.; Randall, J. 2001. Weed control methods handbook: tools and techniques for use in natural areas. The Nature Conservancy. 219 p.

Turner, C.; Center, T.; Burrows, D.; Buckingham, G. 1998. Ecology and management of *Melaleuca quinquenervia*, an invader of wetlands in Florida, U.S.A. Wetlands Ecology and Management. 5(3): 165–178.

U.S. Fish and Wildlife Service. 1999. South Florida multi-species recovery plan. Atlanta. 148 p.

Van, T.; Rayamajhi, M.; Center, T. 2005. Seed longevity of *Melaleuca quinquenervia*: a burial experiment in south Florida. Journal of Aquatic Plant Management. 43(1): 39–42.

Vollmer, J.L. 2005. New technology for fuel breaks and green strips in urban interface and wildland areas. In: Butler, B.W.; Alexander, M.E., eds. Eighth international wildland firefighter safety summit - human factors - 10 years later. Hot Springs, SD: The International Association of Wildland Fire: April 26–28, 2005, Missoula, MT.

Wagner, R.G.; Newton, M.; Cole, E.C. [and others]. 2004. The role of herbicides for enhancing forest productivity and conserving land for biodiversity in North America. Wildlife Society Bulletin. 32(4): 1028–1041.

A comparison of nonfire hazardous fuels treatment options

Fuel treatment	Advantages	Concerns	Potential impacts	Seasonality and intensity of treatment	Application in WUI	Duration of effect	Cost
Mowing	• Reduces shrubs to ground • Turns some fuels into mulch • Encourages herbaceous growth and generally increases species diversity • Requires limited equipment and personnel • Relatively independent of weather • Causes little disturbance to ground cover	• Does not reduce amount of fuel, merely changes structure • Has little impact to roots, so species like palmetto resprout quickly • Unsightly • Difficult to apply with overstory present	• Low risk to public safety, except material can be thrown up to 300 feet from large mowers • May cause some temporary degradation of local air quality from dust	• Can be done in almost any season, but must be done at moderate moisture levels to limit soil disturbance • Intensity is dependent on the size and design of the mower. Larger mowers mulch material better but encounter more obstacles • Can treat up to 10 acres per day	Difficulty depends on the number of obstacles to machinery	3 to 5 years	$40 to $900 per acre
Chipping, disking, and harrowing	• Reduces shrubs to ground • Disrupts resprouting of some shrubs (palmetto) • Encourages herbaceous growth • Generally increases species diversity • Requires limited equipment and personnel • Relatively independent of weather • Harrow exposes bare soil, limiting fire potential until regrowth occurs	• Does not reduce amount of fuel, merely changes structure • Difficult to apply with overstory present • Can disrupt root systems of some desirable vegetation, (e.g., trees) • Unsightly • Harrowing exposes bare soil, increasing potential for erosion and invasive plant colonization	• Low risk to public safety • Significant risk to overstory trees due to root damage • May cause some temporary degradation of local air quality from dust	• Can be done in almost any season, but must be done at moderate moisture levels to limit soil disturbance • Intensity is dependent on the size and design of the chopper, disk, or harrow • Can treat up to 10 acres per day	Difficulty depends on number of obstacles to machinery	3 to 7 years	$70 to $110 per acre
Herbicides	• Can be applied to kill target species or all growth • Easy to apply • Provides long-term impact • Does not physically disturb soil • Limits opportunity for invasive plants • Generally independent of weather	• May encounter public opposition • Does not remove fuel • Creates increased flammability for a period immediately following treat (standing dead fuels)	• May affect nontarget species or overstory trees if improperly applied • May have unknown or unforeseen risks to public health, depending on chemical used	• Must be applied during growing season • Intensity is dependent on chemical and application rates • Can treat up to 15 acres per day	Difficulty based on concern of neighbors, level of toxicity	Up to 10 years	$70 to $110 per acre

continued

43

Appendix 1: A comparison of nonfire hazardous fuels treatment options (continued)

Fuel treatment	Advantages	Concerns	Potential impacts	Seasonality and intensity of treatment	Application in WUI	Duration of effect	Cost
Thinning	• Reduces risk of crown fire by separating trees • May generate revenue • Equipment runs over and compacts shrubs • Minimal soil disturbance • Moderately dependent on weather • Encourages herbaceous growth	• Removes some crown fuel, but does not remove ground-level fuel • May encounter public opposition • Requires proper (moderate moisture) conditions • Creates increased flammability for the period immediately following treatment (slash residue) • Requires >20 acres to generate positive revenue	• Equipment may damage retained trees • May cause some temporary degradation of local air quality (dust)	• Need to avoid excessively wet periods to limit soil disturbance • Intensity depends on volume of tress harvested • Can treat up to 15 acres per day	Difficulty based on site features, concern of neighbors	5 to 7 years	Will produce revenue with enough volume and acreage
Grazing (biomass conversion)	• Defoliates most shrubs from ground up to 5 feet • Converts bulk of live and dead fuel to organic waste • Compacts duff, making it less likely to burn • Encourages herbaceous growth, favoring grasses • Generally increases species diversity • Easy to apply in the presence of obstacles • Minimal impact on nontarget species (trees) and ground cover • Requires limited personnel and equipment • Strong public approval	• Costly on small lots due to animal transportation • Fencing or containment systems are necessary • Few operators are available • Need animal shelter or caretaker near site • Some desirable tree species may be girdled and killed by livestock eating bark • Supplemental mitigation methods may be necessary as livestock may not eat certain flammable plants, e.g., sheep eat saw palmetto but not gallberry	• Very low risk to public safety • Animals may transport invasive plants, diseases, or pest species to site	• Can be implemented most of the year • Intensity depends on objectives: multiple treatments are necessary to kill woody plants; if used with other treatments, periodic grazing can maintain a site indefinitely • Can treat up to 10 acres a day with a large flock	Very useful in most areas, costly in smaller areas	2 to 5 years, depending on vegetation type and number of passes	$200 to $500 per acre; can be used to produce meat or revenue

Source: Florida Department of Community Affairs (2004).

Appendix B:
Resources on prescribed fire

Florida Division of Forestry

John Saddler
Prescribed Fire Manager
Florida Division of Forestry
Telephone: 850–488–9360

Prescribed Fire Councils of Florida

North Florida Prescribed Fire Council
James Furman, Chairman
Eglin Air Force Base
AAC/EMSNP 107 Highway 85 N
Niceville, FL 32578
Telephone: 850–882–8399

Central Florida Prescribed Fire Council
Harry V. Neal, Jr., Past Chair
482 S. Keller Road
Orlando, FL 32810–6101
Telephone: 407–647–7275, ext. 356

South Florida Interagency Fire Management Council
Jon Pasqualone
2401 SE Monterey Road
Stuart, FL 34996
Telephone: 772–288–5633

National Park Service

Big Cypress National Preserve
John Nobles, Fire Management Officer
33100 Tamiami Trail E
Ochopee, FL 34141
Telephone: 239–695–9280, ext. 104

Everglades National Park
David Loveland, Prescribed Fire Specialist
Fire Management Office
40001 State Road 9336
Homestead, FL 33034
Telephone: 305–242–7851

U.S. Fish and Wildlife Service

Fire Ecology Field Office at Tall Timbers
Research Station
Regional Fire Coordinator Office
13093 Henry Beadel Drive
Tallahassee, FL 32312–0918
Telephone: 850–893–4153

U.S. Forest Service

Southern Center for Wildland-Urban Interface
Research and Information
L. Annie Hermansen-Baez
Center Manager/Technology Exchange Coordinator
P.O. Box 110806
Building 164, Mowry Rd.
Gainesville, FL 32611–0806
Telephone: 352–376–3271

The Nature Conservancy

Florida Fire Manager
Zach Prusak
222 S. Westmonte Drive, Suite 300
Altamonte Springs, FL 32714
Telephone: 407–682–3664, ext. 138

Pine Rockland Working Group

Chris Bergh, Chairman
The Nature Conservancy
P.O. Box 420237
Summerland Key, FL 33042
Telephone: 305–745–8402

Appendix C:
Fire management training resources

Florida Center for Wildfire and Forest Resources Management Training

24059 Childs Road
Brooksville, Florida 34601
Telephone: 352–754–6780

Florida Division of Forestry Prescribed Fire Training

Ms. Johnnie Hurst
Hillsborough Community College
1206 N. Park Road
Plant City, FL 33566–2799
Telephone: 813–757–2157
e-mail: jhurst@hccfl.edu

National Interagency Prescribed Fire Training Center

3250 Capital Circle SW
Tallahassee, FL 32310
Telephone: 850–532–8630

Southern Area Wildland Fire Training

Jan Britt
Fire Training Program Manager
U.S. Forest Service
Telephone: 404–347–2595
e-mail: jbritt01@fs.fed.us

Prescribed Fire Councils of Florida

John Saddler
Prescribed Fire Manager
Florida Division of Forestry
Telephone: 850–488–9360
e-mail: saddlej@doacs.state.fl.us

Pesticide Applicator Licenses

Florida Department of Agriculture and Consumer Services
Pesticide Certification Section
3125 Conner Boulevard, Building 8 (L–29)
Tallahassee, FL 32399–1650
Telephone: 850–488–3314

Appendix D:
Endangered animals of pine rocklands and pine flatwoods

Common name	Scientific name	Designated status		Habitat
		FWC	USFWS	Habitat
Amphibians				
Flatwoods salamander	*Ambystoma cingulatum*	SSC	T	F
Gopher frog	*Rana capito*	SSC		F
Reptiles				
Key ringneck snake	*Diadophis punctatus acricus*	T		R
Eastern Indigo snake	*Drymarchon corais couperi*	T	T	F, R
Red rat snake	*Elaphe guttata*	SSC		F, R
Florida brown snake	*Storeria dekayi victa*	T		F, R
Rim rock crowned snake	*Tantilla oolitica*	T		R
Peninsula ribbon snake	*Thamnophis sauritus sackenii*	T		F, R
Florida Keys mole skink	*Eumeces egregius egregius*	SSC		R
Gopher tortoise	*Gopherus polyphemus*	SSC		F
Birds				
Florida sandhill crane	*Grus canadensis pratensis*	T		F
Bald eagle	*Haliaeetus leucocephalus*	T	T	F, R
White-crowned pigeon	*Columba leucocephala*	T		R
Kirtland's warbler	*Dendroica kirtlandii*	E	E	R
Red-cockaded woodpecker	*Picoides borealis*	SSC	E	F, R
Mammals				
Florida panther	*Puma concolor coryi*	E	E	F, R
Florida black bear	*Ursus americanus floridanus*	T		F
Key deer	*Odocoileus virginianus clavium*	E	E	R
Big Cypress fox squirrel	*Sciurus niger avicennia*	T		F, R
Insect				
Miami blue butterfly	*Cyclargus thomasi bethunebakeri*	E		F, R

FWC = Florida Fish and Wildlife Conservation Commission; USFWS = U.S. Fish and Wildlife Service; SSC = species of special concern; T = threatened; F = flatwoods; R = rocklands; E = endangered.
Source: Florida Fish and Wildlife Conservation Commission (2004).

Appendix E:

Flatwoods listed plant species

Species	Scrubby flatwoods	Mesic pine flatwoods	Hydric pine flatwoods
Andropogon arctatus (ST)		X	X
Aristida rhizomophora [a]		X	X
Asclepias curtissii (SE)	X		
Asplenium serratum (SE)			X
Bletia purpurea (ST)		X	
Burmannia flava (SE)		X	X
Calopogon multiflorus [a]		X	X
Campyloneurum angustifolium (SE)			X
C. costatum (SE)			X
Centrosema arenicola (SE)	X		
Cereus eriophorus var. *fragrans* (FE, SE)	X		
Chrysophyllum oliviforme (ST)			X
Clitoria fragrans (FT, ST)	X		
Coelorachis tuberculosa (*, ST)			X
Conradina grandiflora (*, SE)	X		
Ctenitis sloanei (SE)			X
C. submarginalis (SE)			X
Cuphea aspera (*)		X	
Deeringothamnus pulchellus (FE, SE)		X	X
Drosera intermedia (ST)			X
Elytraria caroliniensis var. *angustifolia* (*)			X
Epidendrum rigidum (SE)			X
Eriochloa michauxii var. *simpsonii* (*)			X
Forestiera segregata var. *pinetorum* (*)			X
Glandularia maritima (SE)		X	
G. tampensis (SE)		X	
Gymnopogon chapmanianus [a]		X	
Harrisella filiformis (ST)			X
Hartwrightia floridana (*, ST)		X	X
Hypericum edisonianum (SE)			X
Ipomoea tenuissima (SE)			X
Jacquemontia curtissii (*, ST)		X	X
Justicia crassifolia (SE)		X	
Lechea cernua (*)	X		
L. divaricata (*, SE)	X		
Liatris ohlingerae (FE, SE)	X		
Licaria triandra (SE)			X
Lilium catesbaei (ST)		X	X
Linum carteri var. *smallii* (*, SE)		X	
Lythrum flagellare (*, SE)			X
Microgramma heterophylla (SE)			X
Nemastylis floridana (*, SE)		X	X
Nephrolepis biserrata (ST)			X

continued

Species	Scrubby flatwoods	Mesic pine flatwoods	Hydric pine flatwoods
Nolina atopocarpa (ST)		X	
N. brittoniana (FE, SE)	X		
Ophioglossum palmatum (SE)			X
Panicum abscissum (*, SE)			X
Peperomia glabella (SE)			X
Persea humilis [a]	X		
Phyllanthus pentaphyllus ssp. (*)			X
Pinguicula caerulea (ST)		X	X
P. lutea (ST)		X	X
Platanthera integra (*, SE)		X	
P. nivea (ST)			X
Poinsettia pinetorum (SE)	X		X
Polygala smallii (FE, SE)	X		
Ponthieva brittoniae (SE)		X	
Pteroglossaspis ecristata (ST)		X	
Rhynchospora culixa [a]		X	
R. decurren [a]			X
Ruellia noctiflora (SE)			X
Scutellaria havanensis (SE)			X
Sphenomeris clavata (SE)			X
Spiranthes brevilabris (SE)			X
S. laciniata (ST)			X
S. longilabris (ST)		X	X
Stenorrhynchos lanceolatum (ST)		X	
Stillingia sylvatica ssp. *tenuis* (*)		X	X
Tephrosia angustissima var. *Angustissima* (SE)		X	
Tetrazygia bicolor (ST)			X
Thelypteris sclerophylla (SE)			X
T. serrata (SE)			X
Tillandsia balbisiana (ST)			X
T. fasciculata (SE)			X
T. flexuosa (SE)			X
T. utriculata (SE)			X
T. valenzuelana (ST)			X
Verbena maritima (SE)		X	
Vernonia blodgettii (SE)		X	X
Warea carteri (FE, SE)	X	X	
Zephyranthes simpsonii (ST)			X

S = State; T = threatened; E = endangered; F = Federal; * = U.S. Fish and Wildlife Service, Species of Management Concern.

[a] No designation. Florida Committee on Rare and Endangered Plants and Animals (nongovernment) or Florida Natural Areas Inventory (non-government).

Source: U.S. Fish and Wildlife Service (1999).

Appendix F:
Rocklands listed plant species

Species	Miami Rock Ridge	Big Cypress National Preserve	Florida Keys
Aletris bracteata (SE)	X	X	X
Alvaradoa amorphoides (SE)	X		
Amorpha herbacea var. *crenulata* (FE, SE)	X		
Argythamnia blodgettii (SE)	X		X
Basiphyllaea corallicola (SE)	X		X
Bletia purpurea (ST)	X	X	X
Bourreria cassinifolia (ST)	X		X
Brickellia mosieri (SE)	X		
Byrsonima lucida	X		X
Catopsis berteroniana	X		
Chamaesyce deltoidea ssp. *adhaerens*	X		
C. deltoidea ssp. *deltoidea* (FE, SE)	X		
C. deltoidea ssp. *pinetorum* (SE)	X		
C. deltoidea ssp. *serpyllum* (SE)			X
C. garberi (FE, SE)	X		X
Chamaecrista lineata var. *keyensis* (SE)			X
Chamaesyce pergamena (ST)	X	X	X
C. porteriana (SE)	X		X
Chaptalia albicans (ST)	X		
Coccothrinax argentata (ST)	X		X
Colubrina arborescens (SE)	X		
C. cubensis var. *floridana* (SE)	X		
Crossopetalum ilicifolium (ST)	X		X
C. rhacoma (ST)	X		X
Cynanchum blodgettii (ST)	X		X
Cyperus floridanus (SE)	X		
Dalea carthagenensis var. *floridana* (SE)	X		
Digitaria dolichophylla (ST)	X		X
D. pauciflora (SE)	X		
Dodonaea elaeagnoides (SE)			X
Ernodea cokeri (SE)	X		
Evolvulus grisebachii (SE)			X
Galactia smallii (FE, SE)	X		
Glandularia maritima (ST)	X		
Hypelate trifoliata (SE)			X
Ipomoea microdactyla (SE)	X		
I. tenuissima (SE)	X		
Jacquemontia curtissii (ST)	X	X	X
Jacquinia keyensis (ST)	X		X
Jacquemontia pentanthos (SE)			X
Koanophyllon villosum (SE)	X		
Lantana canescens (SE)	X		
L. depressa (SE)	X		

continued

Species	Miami Rock Ridge	Big Cypress National Preserve	Florida Keys
Linum arenicola (SE)	X		X
L. carteri var. *carteri* (SE)	X		
L. carteri var. *smallii* (SE)	X	X	
Manilkara jaimiqui ssp. *emarginata* (ST)			X
Melanthera parvifolia (ST)	X	X	X
Ocimum campechianum (SE)	X		
Odontosoria clavata (SE)	X		X
Phyla stoechadifolia (SE)	X		
Pisonia rotundata (SE)	X		X
Pithecellobium keyense (ST)	X		X
Poinsettia pinetorum (SE)	X		X
Polygala smallii (FE, SE)	X		
Ponthieva brittoniae (SE)	X		
Psidium longipes (ST)	X		X
Psychotria ligustrifolia (SE)	X		
Pteris bahamensis (ST)	X	X	X
Pteroglossaspis ecristata (ST)	X		
Rhynchosia parvifolia (ST)	X		X
Sachsia polycephala (ST)	X		X
Scutellaria havanensis (SE)	X		X
Selaginella eatonii (SE)	X		
Senna mexicana var. *chapmanii* (ST)	X		X
Smilax havanensis (ST)	X		X
Solanum verbascifolium (ST)	X		
Spermacoce terminalis (ST)	X		X
Spiranthes torta (SE)	X		X
Strumpfia maritima (SE)			X
Stylosanthes calcicola (SE)	X		X
Tephrosia angustissima (SE)	X		
T. angustissima var. *corallicola* (SE)	X		
Thrinax morrisii (SE)			X
T. radiata (SE)			X
Tillandsia balbisiana (ST)	X	X	X
T. fasciculata var. *densispica* (SE)	X	X	X
T. flexuosa (ST)	X	X	X
T. utriculata (SE)	X	X	X
T. variabilis (ST)	X	X	X
Tragia saxicola (ST)	X		
Trema lamarckiana (SE)	X		
Tripsacum floridanum (ST)	X	X	X
Vernonia blodgettii (SE)	X	X	X
Warea carteri (SE)	X		

S = State; E = endangered; F = Federal; T = threatened.

Source: U.S. Fish and Wildlife Service (1999).

Appendix G:

Endemic plant species of pine rocklands

Species

Amorpha herbacea var. *crenulata*
Argythamnia blodgettii
Brickellia mosieri
Chamaecrista lineata var. *keyensis*
Chamaesyce conferta
C. deltoidea ssp. *adhaerens*
C. deltoidea ssp. *deltoidea*
C. deltoidea ssp. *pinetorum*
C. deltoidea ssp. *serpyllum*
C. garberi
C. porteriana
Dalea carthagenensis var. *floridana*
Digitaria pauciflora
Elytraria caroliniensis var. *angustifolia*
Galactia pinetorum
G. smallii
Hedyotis nigricans var. *floridana*
Jacquemontia curtissii
Lantana depressa var. *depressa*
Linum arenicola
L. carteri var. *carteri*
L. carteri var. *smallii*
Melanthera parvifolia
Phyllanthus pentaphyllus var. *floridanus*
Poinsettia pinetorum
Ruellia succulenta
Sabal miamiensis
Sideroxylon reclinatum ssp. *austrofloridense*
Spermacoce terminalis
Tephrosia angustissima
Tragia saxicola

Source: U.S. Fish and Wildlife Service (1999).

Appendix II:
Managers interviewed in preparation of this guide

Name	Title	Agency
Pine rocklands workshop		
Rick Anderson	Fire Ecologist	Everglades National Park, Fire Management
Chris Bergh	Conservation Program Manager, Florida Keys	The Nature Conservancy
Gwen Burzycki	Environmental Resources Project Supervisor	Miami-Dade County Department of Environmental Resources
Chuck Byrd	Land Steward Coordinator	The Nature Conservancy, Florida Keys
Hillary Coolley	Biological Technician	Everglades National Park
Jim Durrwachter	Fire Management Officer-Forester	Florida Panther National Wildlife Refuge
Don Gann		Private property owner
Joyce Gann		Private property owner
Barbara Glancy	Owner/Manager	Pine Ridge Sanctuary
Terry Glancy	Owner/Manager	Pine Ridge Sanctuary
Robin Gray-Urgelles	Biologist I	Miami-Dade County Department of Environmental Resources, Endangered Lands Program
Steven Green	Biologist	The Institute for Regional Conservation
Alison Higgins	Land Conservation Program Manager	The Nature Conservancy, Florida Keys
Tim Joyner	Inspector II Forest Resources Program	Miami-Dade County Department of Environmental Resources
Suzanne Koptur	Professor	Florida International University, Biology Department
Pam Krauss	President	Permitting Assessment and Management, Inc.
Marcos Loperena	Soil Conservationist	U.S. Department of Agriculture, Natural Resources Conservation Service
Anne Morkill	Refuge Manager	U.S. Fish and Wildlife Service, Florida Keys National Wildlife Refuge
Erin Myers	State Biologist	U.S. Department of Agriculture, Natural Resources Conservation Service
Josh O'Connor	Prescribed Fire Specialist	U.S. Fish and Wildlife Service
Erick Revuelta	Biologist II	Miami-Dade County Department of Environmental Resources
Julissa Roncal	Project Plant Ecologist	Fairchild Tropical Botanic Garden
Mike Ross	Associate Professor	Florida International University
Jay P. Sah	Assistant Research Scientist	Southeast Environmental Research Center Florida International University
James Snyder	Research Biologist	U.S. Geological Survey, Florida Integrated Science Center
P.J. Stevko	Forestry Technician	U.S. Fish and Wildlife Service
Sonja Thompson	Restoration Biologist	Miami-Dade County- Natural Area Management
Alberto Vega	Program Director	URS Corporation
Kristie Wendelberger	Field Botanist/Permit Coordinator	Fairchild Tropical Botanic Garden
Dallas Hazelton	Environmental Resources Project Supervisor	Miami-Dade County Parks/ Natural Areas Management

continued

Name	Title	Agency
Pine flatwoods workshop		
Fred Adrain	Administrative Forester	U.S. Fish and Wildlife Service, Merritt Island National Wildlife Refuge
John Aspiolea	Assistant Park Manager	Florida Park Service/Charlotte Harbor Preserves State Park
Kris Brown	Land Management Technician	Brevard County Endangered Lands Program
Brian Christ	Wildlife Technician	Florida Fish and Wildlife Conservation Commission
Roger Clark	Land Steward Manager	Lee County Parks & Recreation
Patricia Cross	Assistant Park Manager	Florida Department of Environmental Protection, Florida Park Service, Hillsborough River State Park
Diana Donaghy	Biological Scientist II (Park Biologist)	Florida Department of Environmental Protection, Division of Parks and Recreation, Myakka River State Park
Keith Fisher	Director, Disney Wilderness Preserve	The Nature Conservancy
William Frankenberger	Natural Resources Liaison	Florida Department of Military Affairs
Jim Green	Land Steward Coordinator	Lee County Parks & Recreation
Laura Greeno	Land Steward Coordinator	Lee County Parks & Recreation
Kraig Krum	Fire Management Coordinator	Palm Beach County/Department of Environmental Resources
Sara Leitman	Environmental Specialist	Alachua County Environmental Protection Department
Christopher Matson	TNC Restoration Projects Coordinator, Disney Wilderness Preserve	The Nature Conservancy
Steve McGuffey	Assistant Land Manager	Brevard County Environmentally Endangered Lands Program
Kelly McPherson	Environmental Specialist	Alachua County Environmental Protection Department
Vince Michault	South Region Assistant Land Manager	Brevard County Environmentally Endangered Lands Program
Clarence Morgan	Rangeland Management Specialist	U.S. Department of Defense, Avon Park Air Force Range
Steve Morrison	Conservation Program Manager, Lake Wales Ridge	The Nature Conservancy
Robert Nelson	Conservation Projects Manager, Disney Wilderness Preserve	The Nature Conservancy
Chris O'Hara	South Region Land Manager	Brevard County Environmentally Endangered Lands Program
Cathy Olson	Senior Supervisor Land Stewardship	Lee County Conservation 20/20
Kris Price	Environmental Lands Foreman	Polk County Board of County Commissioners, Natural Resource Division
Zachary A. Prusak	Florida Fire Manager	The Nature Conservancy
Marcia Rickey	Research Assistant	Archbold Biological Station
Gaye Sharpe	Natural Areas Manager	Polk County Board of County Commissioners, Natural Resource Division
James Snyder	Research Biologist	U.S. Geological Survey, Florida Integrated Science Center
Wayne Taylor	Natural Resource Specialist	U.S. Department of Defense, Avon Park Air Force Range
Karen Vallar	Hydrology Program Manager	U.S. Department of Defense, Avon Park Air Force Range
Sam Van Hook	Kissimmee Valley Forester	U.S. Air Force
Dean Vanderbleek	Fire Manager	Brevard County Environmentally Endangered Lands Program
Tod Zechiel	National Environmental Policy Act Coordinator	U.S. Air Force

Pine rocklands workshop attendees. (photo by Joseph J. O'Brien)

Pine flatwoods workshop attendees. (photo by Joseph J. O'Brien)